John Earle

A Book for the Beginner in Anglosaxon

Comprising a short grammar, some selections from the Gospels, and a

parsing glossary. Third Edition

John Earle

A Book for the Beginner in Anglosaxon
Comprising a short grammar, some selections from the Gospels, and a parsing glossary. Third Edition

ISBN/EAN: 9783337075354

Printed in Europe, USA, Canada, Australia, Japan

Cover: Foto ©Paul-Georg Meister /pixelio.de

More available books at **www.hansebooks.com**

𝕮𝖑𝖆𝖗𝖊𝖓𝖉𝖔𝖓 𝕻𝖗𝖊𝖘𝖘 𝕾𝖊𝖗𝖎𝖊𝖘

A BOOK FOR THE BEGINNER

IN ANGLOSAXON

COMPRISING

A SHORT GRAMMAR

SOME SELECTIONS FROM THE GOSPELS

AND A PARSING GLOSSARY

BY

JOHN EARLE, M.A.

Rector of Swanswick
Rawlinsonian Professor of Anglo-Saxon in the University of Oxford

Third Edition

𝕺𝖝𝖋𝖔𝖗𝖉

AT THE CLARENDON PRESS

1884

CONTENTS.

PREFACE.

THE study of Anglosaxon is the study of a dead language which stands in open continuity with the living English of to-day. It offers a means whereby all who own the English language by birthright may on the easiest terms win a share of those benefits which are more elaborately purchased by the study of Greek and Latin. Truly there is a fine poetic ken which is won by the study of classic languages; but much of this reveals itself spontaneously to the Englishman who will but bestow a look of natural kindness upon the antique glory of his mother tongue. Old language is a sort of poetry. Its poetic light shines out by the foil of modern phrase, and all who vernacularly know the new are qualified to taste the romance that kindles in the old. But while all English folk have a fair inviting gradient between them and the serener heights of Saxon antiquity, the classical scholar has the highest interest in a study which would tend both to increase his usefulness and also to secure to himself the fuller enjoyment of the fruit of his labours.

It will hardly be denied that there is an untoward breach between our academic learning and the general intellect of the land. The education of school and college often perishes because there is no corresponding power of communication. Except in a few favoured spots, its beneficial effects are too obscurely traceable. Might not this be somewhat mended if our more recondite studies were fringed around with a border of native culture, opening a common frontier for barter of thought with the non-graduate world? Might not some of that knowledge which now shrivels for lack of exercise find genial action to the increase of generous thought and the better husbanding of intellectual stores?

In subtle ways of its own English knowledge gives a man surer hold of his distant possessions, and it also enlivens his daily path with glimpses of fresh discovery. Hardly a place, whether in town or country, whether in sheltered nook or open plain, but, either by its name or its dialect, or else by some event, custom or incident, or again by some ancient book or coin or labelled jewel or stone-cut memorial, proffers the cheering stimulant of its homely problems to him who can read writings in Saxon. Whereas he whose knowledge is all remote, stands discontinuous like an alien in his native land.

For the loyal and home-loving Englishman the old Saxon language flings open the gates of learning, and if he have other lore doubles its value — for him the hills and valleys smile with dear associations, transforming the common field into classic ground—for him there is a ready access to the national fountain of poetry, and at least one particular key to the pleasaunce of the faery land.

BEGINNERS BOOK

IN

ANGLOSAXON.

PRELIMINARY NOTE.

ANGLOSAXON is a literary designation for that early
stage of our mother-tongue which was by native usage
in its own day called ENGLISC. This genuine name would
be preferable to any other, and might even now supersede
that of Anglosaxon, but for its proximity of form to the
word English. It is felt that for two conditions of language so divergent as Englisc and English there ought to
be a conspicuous distinction in the names; and this feel-
ing it is that supports the term Anglosaxon[1]. Certainly
this term is not quite un-objectionable. It has been often
urged that by the employment of two names for two
stages of the same tongue, the continuity of the old
language with the new is ignored and obscured. With
some this consideration is paramount, and they prefer
to employ the term English for every stage of the
mother-tongue, from the first colonisation in the fifth
century down to the present day. When this terminology
is adopted, qualifying words are added for distinction of
the great periods, and Anglosaxon is then called 'Old
English.'

[1] This is no modern expression, but one that occurs repeatedly
in some of the best Latin documents of the tenth century.

B

I. ALPHABET.

Anglosaxon manuscripts are written in that form of the Roman Alphabet which had been shapen under the hands of Irish scribes. The letters which are most peculiar in their local form are f, r, s. But in Anglosaxon books, as now printed, there are only two characters unfamiliar to the reader's eye. These are Þ þ and Ð ð. They both represent *th*. The former is the old Rune, called Thorn, and the latter is a modification of the Roman D.

More rarely another Rune, the Wên Ƿ ƿ, is seen in print, chiefly in American books. This is generally replaced by W in the English and by V in the German editions [1].

Sound the vowels after the continental rather than after the modern English fashion. The vowels are a, æ, e, i, o, u, y. These represented in English vocalism would sound as follows : *ah, ae, eh, ee, oh, oo*. The y had a thin *u*-sound, easily confused with the *i=ee*.

C as K; except in so far as ci and ce may have already begun to admit the CH sound.

F for the most part as V. The Latin words *servicium, Vergilius, versus, Vitalis*, figure in Englisc as **serfíse, Fergil, fers, Fiþele**. It was also used for PH, as in **Farisei**, *Pharisees*, **Filip, Orfeus**.

G generally as in *go*. But there was an early softening towards a y-sound, especially before e and i, as in **lufíge**, *I love*, also written **lufíe**.

Give H a gentle guttural sound. Pronounce **niht** neither like *night* nor like *neat*, but something between

---

[1] Some German editors, however, prefer the W, and their number seems to be increasing.

this latter and the German 𝔑𝔦𝔠𝔥𝔱. That the H was very audible may be gathered from the fact that *x* stood as a monogram for *hs*, and it is thus that *next* was formed from **nehst**.

K a substitute for C : perhaps to exclude the CH sound. P is rarely initial. Our list shows but one strong verb beginning with P.

There is no Q. In place of *qu* they used *cw*, and *Torquatus* was rendered **Torcwatus**: but we, when our spelling became romanised, reversed the process and turned **cwén** into *queen*, **cwæð** into *quoth*.

R is guttural and consorts with gutturals. In Greek the initial *ṕ* is aspirated ; and many English words that now begin with R began in Englisc with HR, as **hræfn** *raven*, **hricg** *ridge*, **hreóh** *rough*.

X is a monogram for HS or CS. Thus **acsian** *to ask* is sometimes written **axian**. Even where a word is always written with x in Englisc, the *hs* may be found in another dialect : thus **weaxan** *to wax, grow*, is in Old High German *wahsan* : and **feax** *hair* is in Oldsaxon *fahs*.

Z is no Saxon letter. It occurs only once or twice, and then in foreign names.

II. PRONUNCIATION AND PHONOLOGY.

As the Alphabet is Roman, so we assume that the pronunciation is to be judged in the main by the Roman value of the letters. This is the first of our data for the pronunciation of Anglosaxon. Further light is gained by varieties of orthography. Thus, when **geo** *long ago* is also written **iu**, and **geong** *young* is written **iung**, and **geoguð** *youth* is written **iuguð**, we gather that **ge** before a full vowel had the value of consonantal y. The spelling of modern English contributes something to the evidence. When we observe that **ge** has become *ye*, **gea** *yea*, **gear** *year*, **geard** *yard*, the previous inference is strengthened. We have yet another source in some local pronunciations, where there is reason to believe them to be old. In the North of England the words *light, night* are pronounced gutturally *licht, necht*, and this suggests that the *h* in Anglosaxon was gutturally pronounced.

In Pronunciation there is this chief warning to be given:—Never forget that a silent **e-final** is a thing of recent development! The form *stowe* if met with in Elizabethan English, would be pronounced exactly the same as *stow*: the *-e* has absolutely no value whatever either in sound or in sense, it is a mere thing of orthography. But if in Anglosaxon we meet with **stowe**, it will sound and mean differently from **stow**. The latter is a monosyllable, the former is a disyllable. The Englisc **stow** is a nominative, equivalent to the Latin *locus*; but **stow-e** is a genitive or dative, equivalent to *loci* or *loco* [1].

The vowels demand careful attention; a slight vocalic change in the form of a word will often revolutionize the meaning. Thus **byrnan** is *to burn* as when we say *a wick burns*: but **bærnan** is *to burn* as when we say *the enemy burnt the town.* Traces of these vocalic distinctions remain, as **drincan** *to drink*, **drencan** *to drench*: **feallan**

---

[1] It is hard for an Englishman to acquire a due respect for this -e final in the eldest stage of his mother-tongue. The name of King Ine has to be written in the Latin form of Ina, in order to guard the reader against treating it as a monosyllable. The *rose* is written as in modern English, but in Anglosaxon this is to be pronounced much as the Latin *rosa*; and *lilie* the lily is a word of three syllables.

to fall, fyllan *to fell* : licgan *to lie,* lecgan *to lay* : sittan *to sit,* settan *to set* : windan *to wind,* wendan *to wend* : but more are lost; as búgan *to bow oneself,* bígan *to make another bow* : hnígan *to stoop,* hnǽgan *to make stoop* : lifan *to remain,* lǽfan *to leave* : sincan *to sink* (neut.), sencan *to sink* (act.) : swincan *to toil,* swencan *to slave-drive* : wacan *to wake up spontaneously,* weccan *to rouse another from sleep* : þincan *to seem,* ðencan *to think.*

The simple vowels are seven short, a, æ, e, i, o, u, y; and seven long, á, ǽ, é, í, ó, ú, ý. The distinction between short and long vowels is indicated by the Accent mark upon the long. The Saxon manuscripts suggest this use of Accents, but modern philology has reduced them to system.[1] They are by all means to be studied as a valuable notation, and great sense-differences hinge on them. Thus : ac *but,* ác *oak* : an *on,* án *one* : bær *bore,* bǽr *bier* ; cneow *knee,* cneów *knew* : for *for,* fór *fared* German fuhr : geat *gate,* geát *poured* German goß : hwæte *eager,* hwǽte *wheat* : is *is* German ift, ís *ice* German eiß : lam *lame,* lám *loam* : man *man,* mán *crime* : ne *not* Latin and French *ne,* né *nor* Latin *nec* French *ni* : sæd *said,* sǽd *seed* : tol *toll,* tól *tool* : wende *went,* wénde *weened.* There are two Diphthongs eá and eó. From these must be carefully distinguished the short vowels ea and eo, which are merely modifications of ă and ĭ before a liquid followed by another consonant; thus eald *old* is for ald; meolc *milk* is for milc.

There are two regular systems of vowel-change, discovered by Grimm, and named Ablaut and Umlaut.

Ablaut is an ancient scale of vowel-change upon a, i,

---

[1] Not that the notation is perfectly agreed upon. I propose to mark it (as I understand it) in the Accidence of this manual.

u, which is most conspicuous in the Strong Verbs, as in *sing, sang, sung*.

Umlaut is of comparatively recent date.   It is the change of a vowel in the tonic syllable occasioned by the influence of another kind of vowel in the syllable that is coming.   In the cases which most concern us, the influencing vowel is **i**, and this is the I-umlaut.   The English words *net, fen*, were once *nati, fani* ; the i changed the **a** to **e** and made *neti, feni*; the final vowels fell off, and left *net, fen*.   In the Anglosaxon **here** *army* we have a word in the midway state; it was *hari*: the i has done its work and remains in the enfeebled form of a toneless **e**.   Thus the I-umlaut of **a** is **e** ; of **u** (o) is **y** ; of **á** is **ǽ** ; of **ú** is **ý** ; of **ó** is **ó** ; of **eó** and **eá** is **ý**. This Umlaut is to be observed in the 2nd and 3rd Persons Sing. Pres. Indicative of Strong Verbs (and some of the Weak) ; in the Declension of Nouns, as from **fót** *foot* comes **fét** (=*fóti*), and from **bóc** *book* comes **béc** (=*bóci*).   Also in the formation of some Derivatives; thus from **stán** *stone* an adjective **stǽnen** *of stone*, and a verb **stǽnan** *to stone* [1].

But there are other softenings of vowels which must be kept distinct from the Umlaut.   Such is ·that of **ă** to **ǽ**, which changed the name of Alfred to **Ælfred**.

The vowel **y** calls for a special remark.   There are two distinct kinds of **y**.   The proper **y** is the narrowed **u** (o), whether long or short: thus from **burg** is formed **byrg**, and from **cú** is formed **cý**.   This **y** was (presumably) sounded like German **ü** or French *u*.   The other **y** is umlaut of **ea** or **eo** (long or short) ; and this **y** became

---

[1] And to this day in Somersetshire they talk, not of 'stoning' the roads, but of 'steening' them.

prevalent in the second half of the tenth century [1]. Besides this main distinction, we have to notice what is little better than a confusion between **y** and **i**. The **y** was preferred to **i** (oftener to **ĭ** than to **ī**), simply as a matter of taste and fashion ; so **hym** was written instead of **him**. There are also instances (but they are fewer) of the reverse process ; in which **i** was put for **y** ; as **cining** for **cyning**.

Consonants. The character **y** is never used consonantly in Anglosaxon. This half-consonant sound occurs after **i** before another vowel, and when written it is represented by a **g** ; as **lufige** for **lufie**.

The half-consonant **w** has the like relation to **u** that the half-consonant **g** has to **i**. Nouns in nom. **-u** (**-o**) develop a **w** in oblique cases, thus : **bearu** *wood* gen. **bearwes**, dat. **bearwe** ; **gearo** *ready* nom. pl. **gearowe**.

III. INTERJECTIONS.

The Interjections are either (1) spontaneous and original utterances; or (2) grammatical words lapsed into mere exclamations.

1. Of the first sort are **wá** *wo*, **lá** *lo*, and their composite **wálawá**, out of which have sprung the modern forms *well-a-way* and *well-a-day*.

There is moreover **eála**, which may possibly have had to do with the cry *halloo*. Also **hig** or **he**, *hey, eh, ah, oh, heigh* ; as, **Hig lá me** *Heu mihi*! **Hig Hig, micel gedeorf is hit** *Oh ! Oh ! it is a great toil*.

2. To the second sort belong **efne**, lit. *evenly*, but used

---

[1] Previously, in the Alfredian age, such a vocalism was written ie ; and this orthography has been adopted by some modern grammarians, who prefer **hieran** to **hýran**, **þrie** to **þrý**, **fiend** to **fýnd**, **ieldra** to **yldra**.

as Latin *ecce*, or our familiar *only just look, look you, lo you, mark me.* **Efne we forléton ealle ðing** *Behold we forsook all things.*

Nu *now* is used interjectionally and renders the Latin *ecce*: below, Matt. xxii. 4; xxv. 6.

Hwæt, lit. *what*, but used like 'what ho !' It is a favourite exclamation for the beginning of a poem or of a paragraph. In the following quotation we see it coupled with **lá**, and meaning as much as *hark !* **Suwiað hwæt lá, ne gehyre ge hú myrige lófsangas swegað on heofenum ?** *Hush, hark ! hear ye not how merry hymns resound in heaven ?*

Leof, lit. *dear*, was used as a term of respectful address to a superior, like ' my lord,' ' my liege,' ' Sire,' whether in speech or in the greeting of a letter. The following are the opening words of an epistle from a subject to the king: **Leof, ic ðe cyðe hu hit wæs ymb ðæt lond æt Funtial** *Sire, I declare to thee how it was about the land at Fonthill.* Then it slid into a vague interjectional use, as **Gea leof ic hæbbe** *Yea marry have I* = Etiam habeo: **Ge leof micel gedeorf hit is** = Etiam magnus labor est.

This seems the place for an obscure word **uton**, also written **wuton**, apparently the fragment of a verb, now used as an interjectional conjunction. It governs the infinitive, making it into a hortatory imperative: **wutan cuman ealle** *let us all come*: **wuton cunnian** *let us look sharp*: **uton etan** *let us eat*: **uton faran** *let us set out*: **uton gangan** *let us go*: **uton hleotan** *let us cast lots*: **uton gemunan** *let us remember.*

IV. PARTS OF SPEECH[1].

The Parts of Speech will be found to agree in the main with the analogous parts in English Grammar; but this general correspondence is often broken in detail.

You will often meet with a familiar English word, which yet will not be the same part of speech as the selfsame word is in English. Thus láð in Saxon is an adjective, láð gewidru *foul weather*; whereas in English it is best known as a verb *to loathe*; the adjective surviving only as a relic in the antiquated phrase ' I am loth.'

The word ceáp is the same as the English adjective *cheap*; but in Anglosaxon it is a substantive meaning *cattle*: ge ðæs ceápes ge ðæs cornes *both of the cattle and of the corn*: mid ceápes cwilde ond monna *with murrain of cattle and of men.*

The substantive wyrd *fate* exists in the modern English only as an adjective *weird*.

A more pervading instance is that of the Pronouns hwá *who*, hwilc *which*. In modern English these are both Interrogatives and Relatives; in Anglosaxon they are only Interrogatives and Indefinites.

We may here add a remark upon a change of a different nature. Where the word still lives in English, and still in the same part of speech, it has sometimes undergone a great change in signification. Thus, in Saxon hafoc is a bird of prey, but this word exists in English in a sense widely removed, namely, that of havoc, destruction. For the bird we have adopted the Danish form of the selfsame word, and we call it *hawk*.

These things not only make us feel the distance between Saxon and English; but also they impart a perpetual freshness to the Saxon page, which furnishes for the entertainment of the reader a succession of pleasing surprises.

---

[1] Chapters IV and V are in smaller type, to intimate that the Beginner may pass them over for the present.

V. SYMBOLIC AND PRESENTIVE.

There is a still greater change, viz. that from the Presentive to the Symbolic; from that use of a word in which it stands for a thing or an idea (Presentive), to that use in which it is a pure function of language (Symbolic).

Shall and *will* both exist (as words) in Saxon.   But in that early stage these words meant something widely different from that which they generally mean in modern English. The Saxon **sceal** meant *is due, belongs to* (see Matt. xviii. below), and it is only by filtration through time that *shall, should* have become symbols of Tense and Mood, while the word retains only a film of its original sense of necessity, obligation, and duty.   **Deoſ bóc sceal to Wiogora Ceastre** *This book is to go to Worcester.*

This symbol is used like ſollen in German to indicate that the speaker or writer is only telling something as it has been told to him, without asserting it as a fact.   **Deos wyrt þe man apollinarem and oðrum naman glofwyrt nemneð is sæd þæt Apollo hi ærest findan sceolde and hy Esculapio þam læce syllan** *This herb which they call Apollinaris and by another name Glove-wort; it is said that Apollo should*[1] *first find it, and give it to Æsculapius the leech.*   **Dá he ðá ðider cóm, ðá sceolde cuman þære helle hund ongeán hine, ðæs nama wæs Cerverus, se sceolde habban þrio heafdu.** *When he came thither, there came (as they said) the hound of hell to meet him, whose name was Cerberus; he was said to have three heads.*

The case of *will* is similar.   In Saxon it signified decision and determination of the will ; in modern English, though it has not utterly lost its original power and faculty, yet it is not found once in a thousand times to have any other function than that of a tense-symbol.   So **mæg** *may* in Saxon has to do with *might*, power; and **can** *can* with knowing.

---

[1] This is still, or was not many years ago, good English in Devonshire.

The words dóm, hád, are in Saxon presentive substantives. The meaning of dóm was judgment, decision, choice,
conditions, terms ; and hád meant rank, order, estate, condi-
tion. The first of these is still in English a presentive substantive in the form of *doom*, but in a widely removed sense,
and with a very limited use. If we seek the retreat of. the
Saxon dóm in modern English we find it in the termination
of such words as *Christendom, kingdom, thraldom, wisdom*; not
in a presentive but in a symbolic character.

The case of hád is still more marked. This word has no
existence as a presentive word in modern English. It is now
a symbolic appendage of words in the form of *-hood* : as *boy-
hood, manhood*, a usage which had already begun in Saxon as
cildhád, *childhood*.

Here we see a natural change of the presentive word to
a symbolic use, till it differs little from an inflection. But this
is not the only source of modifying terminations. There are
flectional terminations of which we cannot say that they ever
were presentive words. Such is the famous termination -ing,
which from a vague genitival or adjectival sense (much seen
in Local Names) came to be used as a patronymic ; thus,
Ælfred Æþelwulfing *Alfred the son of Ethelwulf.*

VI. VERBS.

The Verbs form two great Conjugations, the Strong and
the Weak. The characteristic of the Strong Verbs is this, that
they form their Preterite by an internal change of vowel.

1. Of the **Strong Conjugation** three samples follow, in
the verbs brúcan *to use, enjoy*, faran *to go*, wrítan *to write*.

Indicative Pres. sg.	1. brúce	fare	wríte
	2. brýcst	færst	wrítst
	3. brýcð	færð	wrít
pl. 1, 2, 3.	brúcað	farað	wrítað

Indicative Pret. sg.	1.	breác	fór	wrát
	2.	bruce	fóre	write
	3.	breác	fór	wrát
pl. 1, 2, 3.		brucon	fóron	writon

Subjunctive Pres. sg.	brúce	fare	wríte
pl.	brúcen	faren	wríten
Pret. sg.	bruce	fóre	write
pl.	brucen	fóren	writen

Imperative Pres. sg.	brúc	far	wrít
pl.	brúcað	farað	wrítað
	brúce ge	fare ge	wríte ge

Infinitive	brúcan	faran	wrítan
Gerund	brúcanne	faranne	wrítanne
Part. act.	brúcende	farende	wrítende
Part. pass.	brocen	faren	writen

In the Present Tense, notice should be taken of the 2nd and 3rd Persons Singular. The full forms would be *brúc-e-st brúc-e-ð.* We do find such complete forms of many verbs, especially in the poetry; but in prose the more usual is a syncopated form, in which the two syllables are reduced to one; and a change of vowel (often a true Umlaut) has taken place. The *e* which binds the inflection to the stem has disappeared, but its working (it was an ancient *i*) remains in the stem-vowel, where *ú* has become *ý,* and so **brýcst, brýcð.** Luke xi. 10–12.

The Imperative plural **farað** may also be expressed by **fare ge**; and this is but a typical and most ordinary instance of what takes place also in the tenses of the Indicative, namely that if the personal pronoun of the First or Second Person Plural or Dual is put after the verb, its termination drops to -e : **Hwæt is þæt git me sohton?** **nyste git** . . . *What is the reason that ye (two) sought me? Wist ye not . . .?* **Dá becóme wit to anre dene.** *Then arrived we (two) at a valley.*

To this class belong the two great symbol-verbs **wesan** *to be*, and **weorðan** *to become*, German werben.

The Verb *to be* is thus made up :

Present.

		INDICATIVE.		SUBJUNCTIVE.	IMPERATIVE.
Sing.	1.	eom		sý wese	
	2.	eart		sý	wes
	3.	is	weseð	sý wese	
Plur. 1, 2, 3.		{synd / syndon}	wesað	sýn wesen	wesað & wese ge

Present and Future.

Sing.	1.	beó	beó	
	2.	bist	beó	beó
	3.	bið	beó	
Plur. 1, 2, 3.		beóð	beón	beóð

Preterite.

		INDICATIVE.	SUBJUNCTIVE.
Sing.	1.	wæs	wǽre
	2.	wǽre	wǽre
	3.	wæs	wǽre
Plur. 1, 2, 3.		wǽron	wǽren

Infinitive, wesan & beón
Gerund, to beónne
Participle pres. wesende

The parts of this necessary verb are supplied from three different roots; and we shall often see that the words which are most necessary and in most incessant use, are those which exhibit the strangest anomalies.

The verb **weorðan** is conjugated as follows :—

		INDICATIVE.	SUBJUNCTIVE.
Pres. sing.	1.	weorðe	*Sing.* weorðe
	2.	wyrst	
	3.	wyrð	
plur. 1, 2, 3.		weorþað	*Plur.* weorðon
		weorðe we, &c.	
Pret. sing.	1.	wearð	*Sing.* wurde
	2.	wurde	
	3.	wearð	
plur. 1, 2, 3.		wurdon	*Plur.* wurdon
Imper. sing.		weorð	*Infin. pres.* weorðan
plur.		weorþað ⎱	*Gerund* weorðanne
		weorðe ge ⎰	*Part. Past* geworden

The vowel-changes which characterize the Strong conjugation are various in origin, but they nearly all have now the appearance of Ablaut. We know however by comparison with the Mœso-Gothic that a considerable number of these verbs formed their preterites by Reduplication; and a few remnants of Reduplication are still found in Anglosaxon. And even where the Reduplication is no longer extant, the scheme of vowel-change is different in the old Reduplicated Verbs from that of those in which Ablaut seems more original. It is convenient to preserve this distinction in the grouping of our Strong Verbs, because it explains some points of phonology, and also because it is useful in the comparison with other dialects.

Reduplication Groups.

	PRES.	PRET.	PART.
i.	a, ea.	é, eó.	a, ea.
ii.	ǽ.	é.	ǽ.
iii.	á.	é, eó.	á.
iv.	eá.	eó.	eá.
v.	ó.	eó.	ó.

Ablaut Groups.

	PRES.	PRET. SG.	PL.	PART.
1.	i, e, eo(y).	a(o), æ, ea(eo).	u.	u, o.
2.	i, e.	a, æ, ea(e).	á, ǽ.	o, u.
3.	i, e(eo).	æ, ea(a, e).	ǽ, eá(á, é).	e, i.
4.	í.	á.	i.	i.
5.	eó, ú.	eá.	u.	o.
6.	a, ea(y).	ó.	ó.	a, ea(æ, e).

Most of the Strong Verbs extant in Anglosaxon literature will be found in their alphabetical order in the following list. The number prefixed to each verb refers to its Paradigm in one of the above tables. The first column generally exhibits the First Person singular of the Present Indicative. From this form the Infinitive may be inferred, by putting -**an** in the place of the final -**e**. Thus the Infinitive of **beóde** is **beódan**.   •

Pres.	Pret. Sing.	Plur.	Part.	
6. ace	óc	......	......	*ache*
6. ale	ól	......	......	*grow*
6. bace	bóc	bócon	bacen‣	*bake*
i. banne	beón	......	bannen	*summon*
iv. beáte	beót	beóton	beáten	*beat*
· 1. belge	bealh	bulgon	bolgen	*am wroth*
5. beóde	beád	budon	boden	*command*
1. beorge	bearh	burgon	borgen	*keep, secure*
2. bere	bær	bǽron	boren	*bear*
1. berste	bærst	burston	borsten	*burst*
3. bidde	bæd	bǽdon ·	beden	*bid, beg*
4. bíde	bád	bidon	biden	*bide*
1. binde	band	bundon	bunden	*bind*
4. bíte	bát	biton	biten	*bite*
iii. bláwe	bleów	bleówon	bláwen	*blow*
4. blíce	blác	blicon	blicen	*gleam*
1. blinne	blan	blunnon	blunnen	*cease*
v. blóte	bleót	bleóton	blóten	*sacrifice*
2. brece	bræc	brǽcon	brocen	*break*
⎰3. brede	bræd	brǽdon	breden	*braid* ⎱
⎱1. bregde	brægd	brugdon	brogden	*broid* ⎰
5. (a)breóðe	-breáð	-brudon	-broden	*perish*
5. breóte	breát	......	broten	*break*
5. breówe	......	......	browen	*brew*
1. bringe	......	......	brungen	*bring*
5. brúce	breác	brucon	brocen	*use,* brook
5. búge	beáh	bugon	bogen	*bow*
1. byrne	barn	burnon	burnen	*burn*
6. [cale]	......	......	(of) calen	*be cold*
1. ceorfe	cearf	curfon	corfen	*carve*
5. ceóse	· ceás	curon	coren	*choose*
5. ceówe	ceáw	cuwon	cowen	*chew*
4. [cíne]	......	......	(to) cinen	*split*
5. cleófe	cleáf	clufon	clofen	*cleave*

Pres.	Pret. Sing.	Plur.	Part.	
1. climbe	{[clamb]} {clomb}	clumbon	clumben	*climb*
1. clinge	clang	......	clungen	*shrink up*
iii. cnáwe	cneów	cneówon	cnáwen	*know*
3. cnede	......	......	cneden	*mix, knead*
iii. cráwe	creów	creówon	cráwen	*crow*
5. creópe	creáp	crupon	cropen	*creep*
1. cringe	crang	crungon	......	*fall dead*
2. {[cwime]} {cume}	cwom com	cwómon cómon	cumen	*come*
3. cweðe	cwæð	cwǽdon	(ge)cweden	*say*
2. cwele	cwæl	cwǽlon	cwolen	*die*
1. (á)cwince	-cwanc	......	...	*quench,* intr.
1. delfe	dealf	dulfon	dolfen	*delve*
1. deorfe	dearf	durfon	dorfen	*bold out*
6. drage	dróh	drógon	dragen	*draw*
ii. (on)drǽde	{-dreórd} {-dréd} -drédon		[drǽden]	*dread*
5. dreóge	dreáh	drugon	drogen	*endure*
5. dreóse	dreás	......	droren	*fall*
5. (á)dreópe	......	......	dropen	*drop, shed*
3. drepe	dræp	......	{drepen} {dropen}	*kill*
4. drífe	dráf	drifon	drifen	*drive*
1. drince	dranc	druncon	druncen	*drink*
5. (ge)dúfe	-deáf	-dufon	-dofen	*dive*
4. dwíne	dwán	dwinon	dwinen	*pine*
iv. [eáce]	......	......	eácen	*grow*
iv. [eáde]	......	......	eáden	*be happy*
3. ete	æt	ǽton	eten	*eat*
i. fó [fange]	féng	féngon	fangen	*seize*
6. fare	fór	fóron	faren	*go*
i. fealde	feóld	feóldon	gefealden	*fold*
i. fealle	feóll	feóllon	gefeallen	*fall*
1. felhe	fealh	fulgon	-folen	*enter, get in*

C

Pres.	Pret. Sing.	Plur.	Part.	
3. {[feohe]	-feah	-fǽgon }	-fegen	*rejoice*
{(ge)*feó*	-feh	-fégon }		
1. feohte	feaht	fuhton	fohten	*fight*
1. finde	fand	fundon	funden	*find*
5. fleóge	fleáh	flugon	[flogen]	*fly, flee*
5. fleóte	fleát	fluton	floten	*float*
4. flíte	flát	fliton	fliten	*contend*
v. flówe	fleów	fleówon	flówen	*flow*
5. freóse	freás	fruron	froren	*freeze*
3. frete	frǽt	frǽton	freten	*devour*, fret
1. {frigne	frægn	frugnon	gefrugnen }	*enquire*
{frine	fræn	frunon	gefrunen }	
6. gale	gól	gólon	galen	*sing*
i. gange	geóng [1]	......	gangen	*go*
1. gelde	geald	guldon	golden	*pay*
1. gelpe	gealp	gulpon	golpen	*boast*
5. [geópe]	geáp	......	......	*gape*
5. geóte	geát	guton	goten	*pour*
3. gife	geaf	geáfon	gifen	*give*
4. (be)gíne	(to)gán	......	ginen	*gape*
1. (on)ginne	-gan	-gunnon	-gunnen	*begin*
3. (on)gite	-geat	-geáton	-giten	*understand*
4. glíde	glád	glidon	gliden	*glide*
v. [glówe]	gleów	......	......	*glow*
6. gnage	gnóh	gnógon	gnagen	*gnaw*
4. gníde	gnád	gnidon	gniden	*rub*
6. grafe	gróf	grófon	grafen	*dig*
1. grimme	......	grummon	......	*rage*
1. grinde	grand	grundon	grunden	*grind*
4. grípe	gráp	gripon	gripen	*seize*
v. grówe	greów	greówun	grówen	*grow*
i. *hó* [hange]	héng	héngon	hangen	*hang*
iii. háte	héht&hét	héton	háten	*command*
iv. [heáfe]	heóf	heófon	......	*sigh, lament*

[1]. The Preterite in general use is a weak form eóde, from another root.

Pres.	*Pret. Sing.*	*Plur.*	*Part.*	
i. healde	heóld	heóldon	healden	*hold*
iv. heáwe	heów	heówun	heáwen	*hew*
6. [hafe]*hebbe*	hóf	hófon	hafen	*lift*
2. (for)hele	-hæl	-hǽlon	-holen	*conceal*
1. helpe ·	healp	hulpon	holpen	*help*
6. hlade	hlód	hlódon	{hladen / hlæden}	*lade*
iv. hleápe	hleóp	hleópon	hleápen	*leap*
5. hleóte	hleát	hluton	. hloten	*cast lots*
4. hlíde	-hlád	......	-hliden	*cover*
6. {[hleahhe] / hlyhhe}	hlóh	hlógon	[hleahhen]	*laugh*
1. hlimme	......	hlummon	......	*roar*
v. hlówe	......	hleówon	......	*low, bellow*
4. hníge	hnáh	hnigon	hnigen	*bow*
4. hníte	......	hniton	......	*butt, clash*
5. [hreóðe]	hreáð	......	hroden	*furnish, adorn*
5. hreóse	hreás	hruron	hroren	*fall*
5. hreówan	hreáw	......	......	*rue*, impers.˙
v. [hrópe]	......	hreópon	......	*shout*
4. hríne	hrán	hrinon	hrinen	*touch*
1. hweorfe	hwearf	hwurfon	hworfen	*turn*
1. irne[rinne]	arn	urnon	urnen	*run*
iii. láce	leólc, léc	......	......	*sport*
ii. lǽte	lét	léton	-lǽten	*let, leave*
6. leá [leahe]	lóh	lógon	[leahen]	*blame*
5. leóde	[leád]	ludon	loden	*grow*
5. leóge	leáh	lugon	logen	*lye*, lügen
5. (for)leóse	-leás	-luron	-loren	*perish*
3. lese	læs	lǽson	lesen	*gather*
3. licge	læg	lǽgon, lágon	legen	*lie* .
4. (be)life	-láf	-lifon	-lifen	*remain*
4. líhe	......	láh, leáh	......	*lend*
1. limpe	(ge)lamp	-lumpon	-lumpen	*happen*
1. linne	......	lunnon	-lunnen	*cease*

Pres.	Pret. Sing.	Plur.	Part.	
4. líðe	......	......	-liden	*voyage*
5. lúce	leác	lucon	locen	*shut up*
5. lúte	leát	luton	loten	*bend, stoop*
iii. máwe	......	......	máwen	*mow*
1. melte	mealt	multon	molten	*melt*
3. mete	mæt	mǽton	meten	*measure*
4. míge	máh	migon	migen	*mingere*
4. míþe	máþ	......	(be)miþen	*hide, shun*
1. *murne*	mearn	murnon	mornen	*mourn*
5. neóte	neát	nuton	noten	*enjoy*
3. (ge)nese	-næs	-nǽson	-nesen	*recover*
2. nime	nam	námon	numen	*take*
4. nípe	náp	......	......	*grow dark*
2. plion	pleah,pleh......		......	*risk*
ii. rǽde	reórd,réd......		......	*advise*
5. reóce	reác	rucon	rocen	*reek*
5. reóde	......	rudon	......	*redden*
5. [reófe]	......	......	rofen	*cleave,* rive
5. reóte	......	......	roten	*weep, howl*
4. ríde	rád	ridon	......	*ride*
4. (á)ríse	-rás	-rison	-risen	*arise*
v. rówe	reów	reówun	rówen	*row*
6. sace	sóc	sócon	sacen	*dispute*
iii. sáwe	seów	seówun	sáwen	*sow*
6. {scace / sceace}	sceóc	sceócon	sceacen	*move,* shake
6. scafe	scóf	scófon	scafen	*shave*
6. {scape / sceape}	scóp / sceóp} -on		sceapen / scepen	*shape*
iv. sceáde	sceód	sceódon	(ge)sceáden	*divide*
5. sceóte	sceát	-scuton	scoten	*shoot*
2. scere	scær	-scǽron	scoren	*shear*
4. scíne	scán	scinon	scinen	*shine*
4. scrife	(ge)scráf	......	(for)scrifen	*shrive*
1. scrince	scranc	scruncon	scruncen	*shrink*

Pres.	Pret. Sing.	Plur.	Part.	
4. scrîðe	scráð	scridon	scriden	*marcb*
5. scúfe	sceáf	scufon	scofen	*shove*
3. seó [seohe]	seah	sǽgon / sáwon	(ge)segen / sewen	*see*
1. (á)seolce	......	......	(á)solcen	*give up,* sulk
5. seóðe	seáð	sudon	soden	*seethe*
4. síge	sáh	sigon	sigen	*fall*
1. (be)since	-sanc	-suncon	suncen	*sink*
1. singe	sang	sungon	sungen	*sing*
3. sitte	sæt	sǽton	seten	*sit*
iii. slápe, *slǽpe*	slép	slépon	......	*sleep*
6. *sleá* [sleahe]	slóh	slógon	slagen / slægen	*strike, slay*
4. (á)slíde	-slád	-slidon	-sliden	*slide*
4. (to)slípe	-sláp	-slipon	-slipen	*dissolve*
4. slíte	slát	sliton	sliten	*slit*
5. slúpe	sleáp	slupon	slopen	*slip*
5. smeóce	smeác	smucon	smocen	. *smoke*
4. (be)smíte	[smát]	[smiton]	smiten	*defile*, smite
5. sneówe	......	......	......	. *hasten*
4. sníðe	snáð	snidon	......	*cut,* ſchneiden
6. spane	spón / spen	speónon	(á)spanen	*allure*
i. spanne	spén / speón	......	......	*clasp*
1. speorne	spearn	spurnon	spornen	*spurn*
1. spinne	span	spunnon	spunnen	*spin*
4. spíwe	spáw	[spiwon	spiwen]	*spit*
v. spówe	speów	speówon	......	*succeed*
3. sprece	spræc	sprǽcon	sprecen	*speak*
5. (á)spreóte	......	......	-sproten	*sprout*
1. springe	sprang	sprungon	sprungen	*spring*
6. stande	stód	stódon	(ge)standen	*stand*
i. stealde	steóld	......	......	*be well off*
2. stele	stæl	stǽlon	stolen	*steal*

Pres.	Pret. Sing.	Plur.	Part.	
1. (á)steorfe	stærf	sturfon	-storfen	*die*
6. stape, *steppe*	stóp	stópon	......	*step*
4. stíge	stáh	stigon	stigen	*ascend*
1. stince	stanc	stuncon	stuncen	*smell*
1. (of)stinge	-stang	-stungon	stungen	*sting, stab*
3. strede	[stræd	strǽdon	streden]	
1. stregde	strægd	strugdon	[strogden]	*scatter*
5. strúde	......	strudon	(be)stroden	*plunder*
5. súce	seác	sucon	-socen	*suck*
iii. swápe	sweóp	sweópon	swápen	*sweep*
3. swefe	swæf	swǽfon	swefen	*sleep*
1. swelge	swealh	swulgon	swolgen	*swallow*
1. swelle	sweoll	swullon	-swollen	*swell*
1. swelte	swealt	swulton	......	*die*
1. sweorce	swearc	......	(ge)sworcen	*grow dark*
1. sweorfe	......	......	sworfen	*scour, polish*
6. *swerian*	swór	swóron	{[swaren]	*swear*
			{-*sworen*	
4. swíce	swác	swicon	(be)swicen	*fail, betray*
4. swífe	swáf	......	......	*rush*
1. swimme	swamm	swummon	......	*swim*
1. swince	swanc	swuncon	swuncen	*toil*
1. swinde	swand	swundon	swunden	*vanish*
1. swinge	swang	swungon	swungen	*scourge*
v. swógan	......	......	(ge)swógen	*stun, sough*
1. (be)telde	......	......	-tolden	*overspread*
5. teó [teóhe]	teáh	tugon	togen	*draw*
2. tere	tær	tǽron	toren	*tear*
4. [tíhan]	teáh	......	(of)tigen	*accuse*
3. trede	træd	trǽdon	treden	*tread*
5. þeó	þeáh	þugon	(ge)þogen	*thrive*
5. þeóte	þeát	þuton	þoten	*howl*
1. þersce	þærsc	þurscon	þorscen	*thresh*
3. þicge	þeah, þah	-þǽgon	þigen	*taste of*
1. þinde	þand	......	þunden	*swell*

Pres.	Pret. Sing.	Plur.	Part.	
1. [þingan]	......	(ge)þungon	-þungen	*prosper*
iii. þráwe	þreów	......	......	*twist, throw*
5. (á)þreótan	-þreát	......	-þroten	*weary,*imper.
1. þringe	þrang	þrungon	(ge)þrungen *throng*	
1. þrinte	......	......	(á)þrunten *swell*	
6. {[þweahe] / þweá}	þwóh	þwógon	(á)þwegen *wash*	
1. [þweore]	......	......	{[þworen] / (ge)þuren} *weld, forge*	
4. þwíte	......	þwiton	......	*whittle*
6. wace	wóc	wócon	wacen	*wake*
6. wade	wód	wódon	(ge)waden	*wade*
6. wasce	{wócs / wóhs}	wóxon	(ge)wæscen	*wash*
i. wealce	weólc	......	(ge)wealcen *roll*	
i. wealde	weóld	weóldon	(ge)wealden *wield .*	
i. wealle	weól	weóllon	(á)weallen *boil, bubble*	
6. weaxe	weóx	weóxon	(á)weaxen *grow*	
3. wefe	wæf	(á)wǽfon	wefen	*weave*
3. wege	wæg	wǽgon	(á)wegen	*move*
1. weorðe	wearð	wurdon	(ge)worden *become*	
1. weorpe	wearp	wurpon	worpen	*throw*
v. wépe	weóp	weópon	wépen	*weep*
3. wese	wæs	wǽron	[wesen]	*be*
4. wíce	wác	......	......	*yield, give way*
1. winde	wand	wundon	wunden	*wind*
1. winne	wan	wunnon	wunnen	*war, strive*
4. (ge)wíte	-wát	-witon	-witen	*depart*
4. [wite]	wát	witon	witen	*know*
4. wlíte	wlát	wliton	wliten	*look*
3. wrece	wræc	wrǽcon	wrecen	*wreak*
4. wríge	wráh	wrigon	wrigen	*cover*
1. wringe	wrang	wrungon	wrungen	*wring*
4. wríte	wrát	writon	writen	*write*
4. wríþe	wráð	wriðon	wriðen	*wreathe*

This body of Strong Verbs constitutes a sort of ancient core of the mother-tongue; and the student will do well to acquaint himself with them pretty thoroughly. A good plan is to read them frequently and aloud; or even to learn them by heart. But for this purpose they must first be grouped, and it will be easy for the student to do this for himself. If the verbs of any one figure are collected and written in a series, their vocalic harmony will be easily appreciated. The following selection of familiar Verbs from the first Ablaut group may serve for an example:

binde	band	bundon	bunden
ceorfe	cearf	curfon	corfen
delfe	dealf	dulfon	dolfen
finde	fand	fundon	funden
grinde	grand	grundon	grunden
helpe	healp	hulpon	holpen
irne	arn	urnon	urnen
melte	mealt	multon	molten
scrince	scranc	scruncon	scruncen
singe	sang	sungon	sungen
winne	wann	wunnon	wunnen

In all the Ablaut groups but one, there is a change of vowel in those Persons of the Preterite which are disyllables, namely, in the second person of the Singular and the whole of the Plural, as **barn, burne, burnon**[1]; **wrát, write, writon.**

---

[1] The beginner should carefully notice the difference between Strong and Weak Verbs in the Second Person Singular of the Preterite. Thus þu **write** *thou didst write*, but þu **lufodest** *thou didst love*; þu **burne** *thou wast on fire*, but þu **bærndest** *thou didst burn* a piece of paper.

This vowel-change is in certain cases combined with another change, namely, of the last radical consonant. An s is changed to r, and generally a þ to d. Thus the verb ceósan *to choose*, makes preterite ic ceás *I chose*, second person þu cure *thou chosest*, and this -ur- is continued in sequence, viz. we, ge, hi curon *we, ye, they chose*; subj. cure, curen; and coren *chosen*. The same thing happens to the verbs dreósan *to fall*, freósan *to freeze*, hreósan *to rush*, leósan *to lose*. Where the last root-consonant is ð, this is changed in the same parts to d, as may be seen above in weorðan, seóðan.

As the cliffs at Dunwich are eaten away by the sea, and the place is now but a fragmentary monument of ancient celebrity, so the Strong Verbs have been and are continually undereaten by the influence of modern forms. This innovation had already made some way in Saxon times. Just as in the present day the preterite of *sleep* is *slept*, while there coexists a popular Strong form *slepp*, so do we find reversely in good Saxon, that the verb slǽpan pret. slép had already its second preterite in a Weak form slǽpte. There are two preterites of the verb *swear*, namely swór and swerede[1].

Something of the sort happened to the verb *find*, but in a peculiar way. The Strong preterite ran thus, 1. ic fand, 2. þu funde, 3. he fand; but in prose the form of the second person funde gradually prevailed in all three persons. We find ic funde in Luke xv. 6, and he funde in Matt. xx. 6, both among the selections below. A verb that might seem to exhibit the same tendency to transition

---

[1] In the List of Strong Verbs the Italics mark altered, or abnormal, or Weak, forms.—Of Strong Verbs that have subsequently become Weak a list is given in my *English Philology*, § 274.

is **dón** *to do*, which has a Strong Participle **gedon,** with preterite **dyde.** This looks like a weak form, but may perhaps be rather a reduplicate form, and of high antiquity. Other forms of this important Verb are :—*Pres. Ind.* 1. **dó,** 2. **dést,** 3. **déð** ; Pl. **dóð**: *Pret.* 1. **dyde,** 2. **dydest,** 3. **dyde**; Pl. **dydon**: *Imperative* **dó ; dóð ;** *Gerund* to **donne.**

2. The **Weak Verbs** form Preterite and Participle by external addition. There are four types : (*a*) with Infinitive **-an,** Preterite **-de,** Participle **-ed, -d,** or **t**; (*b*) Infinitive **-ian,** Preterite **-ede,** Participle **-ed ;** (*c*) Infinitive **-ian,** Pret. **-ode,** Part. **-od ;** (*d*) Infinitive a disguised **-ian ;** conjugation of mixed features, some of which are after (*a*), and some after (*c*), and some peculiar to itself.

The constituents of these four types being very unequal in numbers, the vast preponderance of the third is indicated by a more conspicuous print. Type-words: **rǽdan** *read*, **ferian** *convey*, **lufian** *love*, **habban** *have*.

Indicative Mood.

		(*a*)	(*b*)	(*c*)	(*d*)
Pres. Sg.	1.	rǽde	ferige	**lufige**	hæbbe
	2.	rǽdest	ferest	**lufast**	hafast &
		rǽtst			hæfst
	3.	rǽdeð	fereð	**lufað**	hafað &
		rǽt			hæfð
Pl.		rǽdað	feriað	**lufiað**	habbað
Pret. Sg.	1.	rǽdde	ferede	**lufode**	hæfde
	2.	rǽddest	feredest	**lufodest**	hæfdest
	3.	rǽdde	ferede	**lufode**	hæfde
Pl.		rǽddon	feredon	**lufodon**	hæfdon

Subjunctive Mood.

Pres. Sg.	ráede	ferige	lufige	hǽbbe
Pl.	rǽden	ferigen	lufigen	hǽbben
	rǽdan	ferian	lufian	hǽbban
	rǽdon	ferion	lufion	hǽbbon
Pret. Sg.	rǽdde	ferede	lufode	hǽfde
Pl.	rǽdden	fereden	lufoden	hǽfden
	rǽddan	feredan	lufodan	hǽfdan
	rǽddon	feredon	lufodon	hǽfdon

Imperative Mood.

Sg. 2.	rǽd	fere	lufa	hafa
Pl. 2.	rǽdað·	feriað·	lufiað·	habbað·
	rǽde	ferige	lufige	hǽbbe

Infinitive	rǽdan	ferian	lufian	habban
Gerund	to rǽdanne	ferigenne	lufigenne	habbanne
Part. Pres.	rǽdende	ferigende	lufigende	habbende
Part. Past	gerǽd	fered	lufod	hǽfd.

(*a*) The first sort has points of agreement with the
Strong Verbs, in the syncope of 2 and 3 Singular Pres.
Indicative, and in the monosyllabic Imperative Singular.
Instead of -de the Preterite has -te after the letters p, t,
and x, as dyppan *to dip* dypte : grétan *to greet* grétte :
lixan *to gleam* lixte : métan *to meet* métte.

In consequence of bringing the -de or -te into im-
mediate contact with the root-syllable, some remarkable
phonetic changes take place in certain cases, as—

cwelle	cwealde	cweald	*kill*
recce	reahte	reaht	*reckon*

syllan	sealde	seald	*give*
stelle	stealde	steald	*place*
telle	tealde	teald	*tell*
þecce	þeahte	þeaht	*cover, thatch*
wecce	weahte	weaht	*wake*
brenge	brohte	broht	*bring*
bycge	bohte	boht	*buy*
réce	róhte	róht	*reck*
séce	sóhte	sóht	*seek*
wyrce	worhte	worht	*work*
þence	þohte	þoht	*think*

Here also belongs the Impersonal Verb (to be carefully distinguished from **þencan** *to think*) **þyncð** *seems*, which makes Preterite **þúhte**, Participle **geþúht**. It is from this Verb that we get 'methinks.'

Some of these form their Imperative Sing. like type (*b*): thus **bige** *buy*, **syle** *give*, **telle** *tell*.

(*b*) Of the second type the verbs are very few: we may name **gebyrian** *befit*, **herian** *extol*, **nerian** *rescue*, **wenian** *wean*, **werian** *defend*.

(*c*) This is the dominant type of the Weak Verbs, and after this type are conjugated all the more recent Verbs, whether formed from native roots or borrowed from Latin.

(*d*) The characteristic of this type is that it has something of (*a*), namely, the syncoped 2 and 3 Sing. Pres. Ind., the Preterite and the Past Participle; and something of (*c*), namely, the Imperative Singular. This type will be easier to understand when we observe that **habban** is for **haflan***; and so **libban** *live*, for **lifian***, with Pret. **leofode**; **secgan** *say*, for **sagian***, with Pret. **sægde**

(sæde) and Imper. Sing. saga (also sege); hycgan *mind,*
for hogian*, with Pret. hogode¹.

There is a Negative of habban, as ic næbbe I have
not, &c.

And here belong twelve **Præterito-Præsentia.** They
are so called, because they start from a Strong Preterite,
which they treat as if it were a Present, and upon it they
build a new Preterite, after the model of Weak Verbs.

	PRESENT.		PRETERITE.	INFINITIVE.	
SG.1&3.	2.	PLUR.			
an	unne	unnon	úðe	unnan	*grant*
can	canst	cunnon	cúðe	cunnan	*know*
þearf	þurfe / þearft	þurfon	þorfte	......	*need*
dear	durre	durron	dorste	......	*dare*
ge-man	-manst	-munon	-munde	-munan	*remember*
sceal	scealt	sculon	sceolde	......	*owe, shall*
mæg	meaht / miht	mágon / mǽgon	meahte / mihte	......	*may*
áh	áge	ágon	áhte	ágan	*own*
wát	wást	witon	wiste / wisse	witan	*I wot*
deáh	duge	dugon	dohte	dugan	*be good for.*
(ge)neah	-nuge	-nugon	-nohte	[-nugan]	*suffice*
mót	móst	móton	móste	......	*may* [must]

We close the Verbs with **willan** *will.* Indic. Pres.
Sg. 1. wile (wille), 2. wilt, 3. wile (wille), Pl. willað (wille
we, &c.). Preterite 1. wolde, 2. woldest, 3. wolde, Pl.
woldon. Subjunctive Sg. wile (wille), Pl. wilen (willen).
The negative form is nyle, nelt, nyllað : Pret. nolde,
noldest, nolden : Subj. nyle, nylen : Imper. nelle þu.

¹ The asterisk attached to a form is now the conventional sign
that such a form is not practically current in the language, but
theoretically made for purposes of explanation.

The Verbs have a strong aspect of antiquity for us moderns, who are used to diminished terminations, such as *loved* for **lufode** or **gelufod,** and the prepositional Infinitive *to love* in place of **lufian** or **to lufigenne.** But with changes of detail everywhere, the main scheme of Strong and Weak and Præterito-Præsentia, is still in outline kept[1], and, after the first novelty, we find with surprise — *How little our Verbs have changed in their Grammar !*

With the Nouns it is different: there we shall see a great and decisive transition.

VII. NOUNS.

In the **Inflection** of **Nouns** we shall have to make acquaintance with a variety of forms which are now extinct : and in fact we here enter upon that part of the grammar in which the mother-tongue wears her strangest aspect, and demands the most minute attention.

Nouns are either (i) Substantives, (ii) Adjectives, or (iii) Adverbs: and the chief thing to be attended to in their inflection is the difference between Strong Declensions and Weak Declensions. This distinction is the main thread to guide us in our exploration of nounal forms.

1.   Declensions of Substantives.

The declensions of the Strong substantives vary with the genders, and therefore the most convenient arrangement for these will be to group them according to their genders: Masculines, Feminines, and Neuters.

[1] Perhaps the boldest exception is that vowel-change in the Persons of the Strong Preterite to which attention has been particularly called.

a. *Strong Declension of Masculines.*

Our type-words for these shall be **smið** *smith*, **fugol** *bird*, **ende** *end*.

Sg. *Nom. and Acc.*	smið	fugol	ende
Dat. and Inst.	smiðe	fugle	ende
Genitive	smiðes	fugles	endes
Pl. *Nom. and Acc.*	smiðas	fuglas	endas
Dative	smiðum	fuglum	endum
Genitive	smiða	fugla	enda

But in **here** *army*, we often find -ig- or -g- inserted between the root and the termination: D. **here** and **herige**, G. **heres** and **heriges**: pl. **herigeas** and **hergas, hergum, herigea** and **heriga.** This -g- represents the consonantal sound produced by -ia-, which was the formative of the stem in certain substantives as in certain verbs, and it is the same as the -g- in **lufige.** Most likely it was pronounced as **y**- consonant.

Besides those of the -ia- stem, there were substantives of -wa- stem: thus **bearu** *forest*, D. **bearwe**, G. **bearwes**: pl. **bearwas, bearwum, bearwa.**

Words with inner vowel **æ** (short) change it to **a** in the cases of the plural: thus **dæg** *day*, makes D. **dæge**, G. **dæges**; but in the plural **dagas, dagum, daga.** So **mæg** *kinsman*, makes **mæge, mæges**; but pl. **magas, magum, maga.**

β. *Strong Declension of Feminines.*

The examples make two groups, according as the substantive ends with a consonant or with the vowel *u* (sometimes *o*): as in the type-words, **gifu** *gift*, **stow** *place*, **læsu** *pasture*.

Sg. Nom.	gifu	stow	læsu
Acc.	gife	stow	læsu
Dat. & Inst.	gife	stowe	læswe
Genitive	gife	stowe	læswe
Pl. Nom.	gifa, -e	stowa, -e	læswa, e-
Acc.	gifa, -e	stowa, -e	læswa, -e
Dat. & Inst.	gifum	stowum	læswum
Genitive	gifa, -ena	stowa	læswa

Those in nom. **-el**, **-en**, **-er**, mostly drop this e in all after cases; as **wylen** *female slave*, **wylne**; **wylna**, **wylnum**. So **swingel** *scourge* makes **swingle**, and **ceaster** *city* **ceastre**. Except substantives in **-ræden**, as **hiw ræden** *family*, **mæg ræden** *relationship*, which make their oblique forms **hiw rædene**, **mæg rædene**; or else **hiw rædenne**, **mæg rædenne**.

Hand *hand* becomes **handa** in dat. sing.; and in nom. acc. plural. Mark vi. 3.

Some have Umlaut forms in the Dative Singular, and in the Nom. Acc. Plural. Such are **bóc** *book*, **bróc** *hose* (*breeches*), **burh** *fort*, **cú** *cow*, **gós** *goose*, **lús** *louse*, **mús** *mouse*, **turf** *turf*.

Sg. N. & A.	bóc	burh	cú
D.	béc	byrg, byrig	cý
G.	bóce	burge	cúe (cús)
Pl. N. & A.	béc	byrg, byrig	cý
D. & Inst.	bócum	burgum	cúum
G.	bóca	burga	cúa, cúna

Of confusion between **burh** and **byrig** be ware;—it is a common source of error. The difference is exhibited in

the following quotation:—and forgeáf him ðá wununge
on Cantwarebyrig, seó wæs ealles his ríces heafod
burh,—*and gave him then a residence in Canterbury which
was the capital of all his kingdom.*

γ. *Strong Declension of Neuter Substantives.*

Here we have two sorts, those which make the plural
nom. and acc. as the singular, and those which take -u
as the sign of plural nominative and accusative. Our
type-words shall be **word** *word*, and **treow** *tree*.

	Sing.	Plur.	Sing.	Plur.
Nom and Acc.	word	word	treow	treowu
Dat. and Inst.	worde	wordum	treowe	treowum
Genitive	wordes	worda	treowes	treowa

1. The first sort are mostly monosyllables ending in a
double consonant, as **hors** *horse*, **land** *land*, **þing** *thing*,
weorc *work*; or having a long vocalism, as **deór** *beast*, **eár**
ear of corn, **leáf** *leaf*, **líf** *life*, **reáf** *garment*, **sceáp** *sheep*,
wíf *woman*. Modern English retains something of this
type in the fact that *sheep* and *deer* have but one form for
singular and plural.

2. The second sort contains neuters with e final in the
Nom. as **ríce** *kingdom* **ríces**; **rícu, rícum, ríca**:—
disyllables in **er** (or), **el** (ol), **en,** and they contract when
they receive case-endings, as **wundor** *wonder*, **wundre,**
wundres ; wundru, wundrum, wundra :—monosyllables with short vowel and simple consonant. Thus
god was an old neuter substantive in heathen times, and
made pl. **godu**; but under Christianity it became masculine for God, and from this was formed a masculine
plural **godas**; it did not however immediately banish
the old neuter plural **godu**, which still was long used

as a distinct expression for the gods of the heathen. Words with æ before a single end-consonant, turn æ to a before the endings -u, -a, -um: as fæt *vat, vessel,* fæte, fætes; fatu, fatum, fata; wæl *slaughter,* plural walu.

§ *Some Anomalies in the Strong Substantives.*

Some common words are peculiar. Thus sunu *son,* makes D. and G. suna, pl. N. suna, D. sunum, G. suna and sunena. In the same manner wudu *wood,* sidu *custom;* and the fem. duru *door.*

Then broðor (-er) *brother,* makes G. broðor, D. breðer; pl. N. broðra (u), D. broðrum, G. broðra. And dóhtor *daughter,* makes G. dóhtor, D. déhter; sweostor *sister,* D. swyster pl. swustra. We must note likewise the collective plurals gebróðor (-ru) *brethren,* gesweostor, like the German Gebrüder, Geſchwiſter. The word fæder *father* is often undeclined in the sing. (G. fæderes is found); but in pl. like smið. And módor *mother,* makes G. módor and méder, D. méder.

The word man *man,* makes D. men, G. mannes: pl. N. menn, D. mannum, G. manna. There is a rare Acc. Sing. mannan or monnan. In like manner fót *foot,* pl. fét; tóð *tooth,* pl. téð.

Freónd *friend,* and feónd *enemy,* are like smið in other respects:—but they form pl. nom. and acc. thus, frýnd, fýnd. Also the dat. sg. is frýnd.

The word for *stream* eá (M. and F.), mostly indecl. in Sing., has a Gen. eás; Pl. Dat. eám. The word for *sea* sǽ, mostly indecl. in Sing., has a Gen. sǽs, and a rare Dat. sǽwe; Pl. Dat. sǽm. The word *shoe* scóh makes

G. scós; Pl. strong and weak, scós and scón. Four neuters **æg** *egg*, **cealf** *calf*, **cild** *child*, **lamb** *lamb* have plurals in -u with inserted -er-; **ægru, cealfru, cildru, lambru.** But oftenest the pl. of **cild** is the unaltered word, according to the ordinary rule for neuter substantives.

ℵ. *The Weak Declensions of Substantives.*

These differ so little from one another, that the three genders may be taken together, and exhibited in one frame, thus:

	MASC.	FEM.	NEUT.
Nom.	-a	-e	-e
Acc.	-an	-an	-e
Dat. Instr. and Gen.	-an	-an	-an

Nom. and Acc.	-an
Dat. and Instr.	-um
Genitive	-ena

The three type-words, Masc. **steorra** *star*; Fem. **tunge** *tongue*; Neut. **eáge** *eye*, may be conveniently declined in one table:

		MASC.	FEM.	NEUT.
Sing.	*Nom.*	steorra	tunge	eáge
	Acc.	steorran	tungan	eáge
	Dat. Instr. and Gen.	steorran	tungan	eágan
Plur.	*Nom. and Acc.*	steorran	tungan	eágan
	Dat. and Instr.	steorrum	tungum	eágum
	Genitive	steorrena	tungena	eágena

But, while we tabulate the three genders as if on equal terms, it must be noted, that the Weak forms are almost all masculine or feminine; of Neuters we can muster but one or two examples besides the type-word, namely, **eáre** *ear*, and perhaps **lunge** *lung*.

§ *Proper Names.*

Men's Names are mostly strong, as Ælfred G. Ælfredes, but some are weak, as **Offa** G. **Offan**. Women's Names are mostly strong, as **Ælfgifu** G. **Ælfgife** : under Latin influence some are weak, as **Marie** G. **Marian**. Nations' Names are mostly strong, in -e (an old -i) as **Angle, Angla, Anglum**; **Dene, Dena, Denum**; **Suþrige, Suþrigea, Suþrigum**; but **Seaxe** has Gen. of weak type **Seaxena**.

2.   Declension of Adjectives.

The **Adjectives** are not, like the substantives, subject merely to one or other of the two schemes of variation called Strong and Weak, but each adjective is liable, according to circumstances which will be explained in the Syntax, to both sorts of inflection. Here it will be sufficient to note, as the most ordinary instrument of the distinction, that the adjective with the definite article takes the Weak, without it the Strong formation. These different sets of forms are here exemplified in the type-word **gód** *good.*

Strong.

		MASC.	FEM.	NEUT.
Sing.	*Nom.*	gód	gód	gód
	Acc.	gódne	góde	gód
	Dat.	gódum	gódre	gódum
	Instr.	góde	......	góde
	Gen.	gódes	gódre	gódes

Plur.	*Nom. and Acc.*	góde
	Dat.	gódum
	Gen.	gódra

Weak.

	MASC.	FEM.	NEUT.
Sing. Nom.	(se) góda	(seó) góde	(ðæt) góde
Acc.	(ðone) gódan	(ðá) gódan	(ðæt) góde
Dat.	(ðam) gódan	(ðǽre) gódan	(ðam) gódan
Gen.	(ðæs) gódan	(ðǽre) gódan	(ðæs) gódan

Plur. Nom. and Acc.	(ðá) gódan	
Dat.	(ðám) gódum	
Gen.	(ðára) gódena	

Care must be taken to distinguish between the -e of oblique flexion, and a nom. -e of some adjectives, as blíðe *blithe*, céne *keen*, clǽne *clean*, deóre *dear*, éce *everlasting*, gréne *green*, mǽre *splendid*, ríce *rich*, swéte *sweet*.

Participles are declined like adjectives both definitely and indefinitely, except that in the weak gen. pl. they keep to -ra; thus, not þara rihtwillendena, which would be too draggling, but þara rihtwillendra *of the upright*: þara ungelæredra *of the unlearned*: þæra gehyrendra heortan awehte *he stirred the hearts of the hearers*. This seems to be matter of euphony, for it is not the part of speech that determines it, but the length of the word. We also find þæra Egyptiscra *of the Egyptians*, þæra hæðenra *of the heathen*.

The participle is first an adjective, but it easily becomes a substantive; and according as the Present Participle assumes one or other of these two characters, it has a different declension[1]. Let us compare the strong masculine declension of the adjectival wegferende *wayfaring* with that of the substantival wegferend *a wayfaring man*.

---

[1] When Hælend *healing* was adopted as an equivalent for the name JESUS, it was at first declined as an Adjective, but afterwards as a Substantive.

		ADJECTIVE.	SUBSTANTIVE.
Sing.	*Nom.*	wegferende	wegferend
	Acc.	wegferendne	wegferend
	Dat.	wegferendum	wegferende
	Gen.	wegferendes	wegferendes
Plur. Nom. and Acc.		wegferende	wegferendas
	Dat.	wegferendum	wegferendum
	Gen.	wegferendra	wegferenda

Gif þu lufast þás woruld, heó besencð þe, forðam ðe heó ne cann áberan hire lufigendas, ac cann bepæcan *If thou lovest this world, she will sink thee, because she knows not how to support her lovers, but does know how to deceive.*

The Comparative Degree of Adjectives.

The distinction between forms Strong and Weak takes in this place a decisive and significant line of action. The Strong Comparative, as **heardor** *harder*, is used only as an Adverb. When the Comparative is Adjectively used, whether in concord with a substantive or not, then it has only one form, and that the Weak, namely, **heardra, heardre, heardre.**

There is in this a logical propriety of which we will speak in the Syntax. In this place we ask the reader to master the fact and make himself familiar with it, by the aid of the following illustrations :—

Singular.

Nom.   *Masc.* **Se stranga . . . . gyf þonne strengra ofer hine cymð** *The strong man . . . . if then a stronger cometh upon him.*

Neut. Þæt is cúðre líf *That is a nobler life.*

Accus. Masc. Næfre ic geférde heardran drohtnoð
Never did I light upon harder fortune.

Fem. Ic hæbbe maran gewitnesse *I have greater witness.*

Plural.

Nom. Ge synd sélran þonne manega spear-
wan *Ye are better than many sparrows.*
Þa wæron ægðer ge swiftran ge
unwealtran ge eac hiéran þonne
þa oðru *They were both swifter and
less rolling and eke higher than the
others.*

The Superlative Degree.

Here the twofold system returns, and the Superlatives,
like the Positives, have in their adjectival capacity, both
the Strong and Weak declensions. In the Strong declension the termination is -ust, -ost, -est; in the Weak it
is -osta, -oste; or -esta, -este.

Þes is mín leófesta sunu *This is my dearest son.*

Þá hæfde he þá gyt ánne leófestne sunu *Then
had he yet one most beloved son.*

Þá men þe swiftoste hors habbað *The men that
have swiftest horses.*

Here as elsewhere some of the commonest and most
necessary words have peculiarities of form; and the
beginner will find it useful in reading to refer often to the
following lists.

Anomalous Comparison.

Some of the most frequent and indispensable words have peculiar modes of comparison.

(1) Some exhibit a patchwork of divers roots, as—

	POSITIVE.	COMPARATIVE.	SUPERLATIVE.
good	gód (wel)	betera (bet)	betst
bad	yfel	wyrsa (wyrs)	wyrrest, wyrst
great	{micel}{fela}	mára (má)	mæst
little	lytel (lyt)	læssa (læs)	læst

The bracketed forms are adverbial.

(2) Some suffer vowel-change, as—

old	eald	ieldra, yldra	ieldest, yldest
easy	eáð	(eð)	eáðost
young	geong	gyngra	gyngest
high	heáh	hiera, heárra, hérra	héhst
nigh	neáh	(neár)	néhst, next
short	sceort	scyrtra	scyrtest
long	lang	lengra (leng)	lengest

The usual rule, whereby adverbs are the offspring of adjectives, seems reversed in the following list, where we see instances of words which are only adverbs or prepositions in the Positive, become adjectival in the higher degrees :—

ere	(ǽr)	ǽrra (æror)	ǽrest (ærost)
after	(æfter) afterweard	æftera	æftemest
fore	(fore) foreweard	....	forma, fyrmesta
forth	(forð)	(furðor)	(furðum ?)
kind	(hindan)	(hinder)	hindema
in	(inn) inneweard	innera	innema, innemest
mid	(mid) middeweard	....	midmest

north (norð) norðweard (norðor)		norðmest
nether niðeweard	niðera (niðor)	niðemest
up ufeweard (ufan)	ufera (ufor)	yfemest
out (út) úteweard	(útor) úterra, ýtra	ýtemest

The Superlatives in -m-est are cumulate forms; an ancient Superlative in -ma having been treated as if it were a Positive, and then rendered subject to the later rule of comparison, by the addition of -est.

The ancient Superlative -ma has only the Weak declension; but the later -mest has both the Strong and the Weak, as :—þa fyrmestan ytemeste, and þa ytemestan fyrmeste *The first last, and the last first.*

3. Formation of Adverbs.

The most frequent formative of Adverbs is the flectional termination -e added to the stem of the Adjective; thus from the adjective swið *vehement,* is formed the adverb swiðe *vehemently,* exceedingly, as swiþe gewundod *seriously wounded;* he wæs swiðe wáclic on his gewǽdum *he was very mean in his attire.* This swiðe became the trite and common adverb of every-day use, corresponding to our ' very,' and it may be met with ten times in a page.

The Comparative degree is simply in -or as swiðor; the Superlative in -ost as swiðost.

The adjectives and adverbs are so closely knit into one system, that they may conveniently be tabulated together.

	POSITIVE.	COMPARATIVE.	SUPERLATIVE.
Adj. Strong	swið	......	swiðost
Adj. Weak	swiða, -e	swiðra, -e	swiðesta, -e
Adverb	swiðe	swiðor	swiðost

Example of the Adverb swíðe in each Degree :—

Positive. And þa swíðe raþe æfter þæm *And then very
soon after that.*

Comp. Hit wyrsode swíðor and swíðor *It grew
worse and worse.*

Superl. Folces frið bette swíðost þara cyninga *He
bettered the folk's peace most effectually of the
kings.*

In the following quotation this adverb appears in all the
three degrees. Næfde se here, Godes þonces, Angel
cyn ealles for swíðe gebrocod: ac hie wæron micle
swíþor gebrocede on þæm þrim gearum mid
ceapes cwilde and monna: ealles swíþost mid þæm
þæt manige þara selestena cynges þena þe þær on
londe wæron, forð ferdon on þæm þrym gearum.
*The invading host had not, thank God, distressed the English
nation so very severely; but they were much more distressed
during the three years with murrain of cattle and of men;
worst of all by the fact that many of the best of the king's
thanes that were in the land died in the course of that three
years.*

But the place where this -e most largely figures, is in
the adverbializing of adjectives in -lic : sóðlic *true-like,*
sóðlice *soothly, truly.* Hence the -*ly* of our prevalent
modern adverb.

Other Adverb formatives are in -**inga**, -**unga**, as :

> dearninga *clandestinely.*
> eáwunga *openly.*
> færinga *suddenly.*
> holinga *in vain.*
> hraðinga *swiftly.*

irringa *wrathfully.*
neádinga *of necessity.*
orsceattinga *gratuitously.*
semninga *suddenly.*
unceápunga *gratuitously.*
wénunga *conceivably.*

In -um, as medmiclum *moderately,* Nyttigen baþes medmiclum *Let them use the bath moderately.*

In -an, as niwan *newly :* Nis þeos lár niwan aræred *This doctrine is not newly set up.*

The termination -an has the sense of *from,* like the Greek θεν in ἔξωθεν *from without,* οὐράνοθεν *from heaven.* Like these are foran *in front,* innan *within,* útan *from outside,* æftan *from behind,* feorran *from far,* neán *from near,* niðan *from below.* The points of the compass eást, west, norð, suð, have their Adverbs of direction eástan, westan, norðan, súðan. The rage of the Danes against Abp. Ælfheah is partly accounted for by the chronicler thus :—Wæron hi eac swyðe druncene, forþam þær wæs ge broht wín súðan *Also they were very drunk, for wine was brought there from the south.* This form is frequent among the Prepositions.

§ The Numerals.

Numerals are either Cardinal or Ordinal, and both are subject to declension. The Cardinals have a fitful and fragmentary declension ; the Ordinals a steady and regular one. But the leading distinction between them is the same as that which we have found so guiding in substantives, adjectives, and adverbs. It is the distinction between Strong and Weak. The Cardinals decline Strong ;

the Ordinals decline Weak. The only exception is **ó𝛿er** which declines Strong. An apparent, but not real, exception is **ána,** a weak form of **án.** But **ána** is rather a Pronoun than a Numeral, as *unus* is in ·Latin when employed in the sense of *solus* : **God ána wát** *God only knows,* Deus unus scit : **and he ána wæs on lande** *and he alone was on land,* et ipse solus in terra.

	CARDINALS.	ORDINALS.
1	án	forma, -e
2	twegen, twá	ó𝛿er
3	þrý, þreó	þrídda, -e
4	feówer	feór𝛿a
5	fíf	fífta
6	six (siex)	sixta
7	seofon	seofo𝛿a
8	eahta	eahto𝛿a
9	nigon	nigo𝛿a
10	týn	teó𝛿a
11	endlufon	endlyfta
12	twelf	twelfta
13	þreótýne	þrýteó𝛿a
14	feówertýne	feowerteó𝛿a
15	fíftýne	fífteó𝛿a
16	sixtýne	sixteó𝛿a
17	seofontýne	seofonteó𝛿a
18	eahtatýne	eahtateó𝛿a
19	nigontýne	nigonteó𝛿a
20	twéntig	twéntigo𝛿a
21	án and twéntig	án and twéntigo𝛿a
22	twá and twéntig	twá and twéntigo𝛿a
30	þrittig	þrittigo𝛿a

40	feówertig	feówertigoða
50	fíftig	fíftigoða
60	sixtig	sixtigoða
70	(hund-)seofontig	hund-seofontigoða
80	(hund-)eahtatig	hund-eahtatigoða
90	(hund-)nigontig	hund-nigontigoða
100	hundteóntig hund, *hundred*	hund-teóntigoða
110	hund-endlufontig .	·
120	hund-twelftig	
200	twá hund	
1000	þúsend	
2000	twá þúsendo	

The acc. sing. masc. of the Strong form **ánne**, is oftener written **énne**. For **án** is declined like an adjective, with the three genders, just as *unus* is in Latin. The same thing happens partially to the second and third Cardinals.

	MASC.	FEM.	NEUT.	MASC.	FEM.	NEUT.
N. and A.	twégen	twá	twá (tú)	þrý	þreó	þreó
D.	twám (twǽm)			þrím		
G.	twegra (twega)			þreóra		

Other Cardinals are occasionally declined: **ealle butan fífum** *all but five*, and see Mark iv. 12 **þa twelfe** *the Twelve.*

Like **twá** is declined M. **begen**, F. **bá**, N. **bá (bútú)** *both.*

For the first Ordinal, besides **forma,** there are the words **fyrresta, fyrsta, formesta, fyrmesta,** and **ǽresta.**

In the Adverbial expression of Numbers, the first three Numerals have a form of their own, **ǽne** *once,* **twíwa (túwa)** *twice,* **þríwa** *thrice.* The other numeral adverbs are formed by the help of **síðe,** instrumental case sing. of síð *journey, time,* added to Ordinals; as þriddan síðe *the third time,* sume síðe *some time, once on a time.* Or with síðum (síðon) instr. pl. added to Cardinals, as feower síðon *four times.*

VIII. PRONOUNS.

The student is advised to give minute attention to the **Pronouns.** There are some distinctive features which might the more easily escape nótice, because of a rough general similarity between the Saxon and the English Pronouns.

The Pronouns fall into six groups, (1) Personal, (2) Possessive, (3) Demonstrative, (4) Relative, (5) Interrogative, (6) Indefinite.

1. The **Personal Pronouns** of the First and Second Persons are without distinctions of Gender, but they have three Numbers :—

		FIRST PERSON.	SECOND PERSON.
Sing.	*Nom.*	ic *I*	þu *thou*
	Acc.	(meh, mec) me *me*	(þec) þe *thee*
	Dat.	me *to or for me*	þe *to or for thee*
	Gen.	mín *of me*	þín *of thee*
Dual	*Nom.*	wit *we two*	git *ye two*
	Acc.	(uncit) unc *us two*	(incit) inc *you two*
	Dat.	unc *to or for us two*	inc *to or for you two*
	Gen.	uncer *of us two*	incer *of you two*
Plur.	*Nom.*	wé *we*	gé *ye*
	Acc.	(úsic) ús *us*	(eówic) eów *you*
	Dat.	ús *to or for us*	eów *to or for you*
	Gen.	(úser) úre *of us*	eówer *of you*

The bracketed forms are archaic. A fine example of MEC may be seen in the legend on Alfred's Jewel

AELFRED MEC HEHT GEWYRCAN, *Alfred ordered to make me*[1]. The Pronoun of the Third Person has three Genders in the singular :—

Singular.

	MASC.	FEM.	NEUT.
Nom.	he *he*	heó *she*	hit *it*
Acc.	hine *him*	hí *her*	hit *it*
Dat.	him *to him*	hire *to her*	him *to it*
Gen.	his *his, of him*	hire *her, of her*	his *its*

Plural.

FOR ALL GENDERS.

Nom. and Acc.	hí, hie, hig, hio, *they, them*
Dat.	him, heom *to them*
Gen.	hira, heora *of them, their*

This Third Personal Pronoun was anciently a Demonstrative, and there are certain adverbs which grew out of it when it was in that stage, which adverbs retain their original demonstrative force, namely **her** *here*, **hider** *hither*, **heonan** *hence*, to be noticed again below, under Adverbial Pronouns.

2. The **Possessive Pronouns** of the First and Second Persons are based upon the Genitives of their respective Personal Pronouns, which then decline as ·adjectives, namely, **mín** *mine, my* ; **uncer** *our* (dual), **úre** *our* (pl.) ; **þín** *thine, thy,* **incer** *your* (dual), **eówer** *your* (pl.). These are declined strong as adjectives. Thus **úres cynges fæder** *our king's father* : **eówre geferan** *your companions.*

---

[1] This noble relic is in the Ashmolean Museum, and should be visited by the student who lives within reach of it.

There is no adjectival Possessive Pronoun of the Third person, but the simple genitives **his** *his*, *its*, **hire** *her*, **hira**, **heora** *their*, serve this purpose just as in modern English.

3. The **Demonstrative Pronouns** are *this* and *that*, just as now, only they have Genders and Cases

	That.			*This.*		
	MASC.	FEM.	NEUT.	MASC.	FEM.	NEUT.
Sg. N.	se	seó	þæt	þes	þeós	þis
A.	þone	þá	þæt	þisne	þás	þis
D.	þǽm	þǽre	þǽm	þisum	þisse	þisum
Instr.	þý, þé (þon)	...	þý, þé (þon)	þýs	...	þýs
G.	þæs	þǽre	þæs	þisses	þisse	þisses
Plur. N. and A.	þá			þás		
D.	þám, þǽm			þisum		
G.	þára, þǽra			þissa		

Observe the distinct form for the case which we may call Instrumental or Ablative or Locative, for which a form distinct from the Dative is clearly displayed in the case of **þý**. It is much used in the Saxon Chronicles.

And þý ilcan geare sende Æþelwulf cyning Ælfred his sunu to Rome *And in that same year king Ethelwulf sent Alfred his son to Rome.*

In the above we see the Demonstrative use in full action. But the prevalent use of **se—seo—þæt** is in the character of a Definite Article, and it is this fact which invests this Demonstrative with its great importance in Anglosaxon.

Example of Genitive Singular Feminine of **þis** :—

Ælfred cyning wæs wealhstod þisse béc *King Alfred was the translator of this book.*

To this group belong three adverbial pronouns of locality—þær *there*, þider *thither*, þonan *thence* : to be noticed again below, under Adverbial Pronouns.

4. Of **Relative Pronouns** there is only one form which is distinct and separate from other pronouns, and that is the indeclinable þe : þæt micele geteld þe Móises worhte *The great tent which Moses made.*

I who am	ic þe eom
thou who art	þu þe eart
he who is	se þe is

not the 3 Pers. Pronoun (not *he þe*) but the Demonstrative : sý gebletsod se þe com on Drihtnes naman *blessed be he that ath come in the Lord's name* : oncnáwað þone þe ge geseoð *recognize him whom ye see.* Gradually however the Demonstrative entered so deep into the office of the Relative, that þe was often set aside, and the commonest way was to repeat the Demonstrative, using it first as Antecedent and next as Relative. Thus se . . . se *he who*, þæt . . . þæt *that which.* Se man se þæt swifte hors hæfð *The man who hath the swift horse.*

5. The **Interrogative Pronouns** are three, all of an adjectival kind, furnishing forth the three questions :—

a. *Who* and *What?*

N.	hwá	hwæt
A.	hwone	hwæt
D.	hwǽm	hwam
G.	hwæs	hwæs
Inst.	......	hwý

E

b. *Which of two ?*

		MASC.	FEM.	NEUT.
Sing.	*N.*	hwæðer	hwæðeru	hwæðer
	A.	hwæðerne	hwæðere	.hwæðer
	D.	hwæðerum	hwæðerre	hwæðerum
	G.	hwæðeres	hwæðerre	hwæðeres
Plur.	*N.* *A.*	hwæðere	hwæðere	hwæðeru
	D.	hwæðerum	hwæðerum	hwæðerum
	G.	hwæðerra	hwæðerra	hwæðerra

c. *What sort of ?* or *Which of all ?* is expressed by
hwilc (hwelc, hwylc), and this is declined like any
strong adjective.

Of an adverbial kind, three of locality; **hwær** *where,*
hwider *whither,* **hwonan** *whence* : one of time **hwænne**
when : one modal **hú** *how ?*

6. The **Indefinite** Pronouns are a very diversified
group.

Some of them are taken from the Interrogatives. Thus
hwá is not only *who ?* but also *some one, any one* : and
hwæt *somewhat, something* ; as, **hwæt lytles** *some little* ;
and **hwylc** *one, any one* ; **swa fram slæpe hwylc arise**
as if one rose from sleep.

These combine with **swa** to make composite pronouns,
as **swa hwa swa** *whosoever* ; **swa hwæt swa** *whatsoever* ;
swa hwilc swa *whichsoever.*

And **hwilc** makes with **swa** a composite Indefinite
which has prepared the way for the later *whichsoever.*
Þider urnon, swa hwilc swa þonne gearo wearð
Thither they ran, whichsoever then ready was.

Again, Interrogatives form Indefinites by taking the
prefix **æg-** or **ge-** ; as **æghwá, æghwæt, æghwilc,**

ǽghwæðer (ǽgðer), gehwá, gehwǽt, gehwilc, gehwǽðer *whoever, whatever, whichever, both of the two.* Especially **gehwilc** is eminently useful by reason of its vagueness, which is the cardinal virtue of an Indefinite Pronoun. It can mean upon occasion any of these : *each one, every one, many a one, some folk, certain, divers, various* : **And hiera se æðeling gehwelcum feoh and feorh gebead, and hiera nænig hit geþicgean nolde** *And the Prince offered to each one of them money and life, and not any one of them would touch it.* **Gehergade swiðe micel on þæm norð here, ægðer ge on mannum ge on gehwelces cynnes yrfe** *Harried very much on the north army, both on men and on every kind of cattle.* **Augustinus gesette biscopas of his geférum gehwilcum burgum on Engla þeode** *Augustine set bishops from among his companions to divers cities in the English nation.*

Sum answers but partially to our *some.* It is very like the Greek τίς, and will require various turns of rendering, *one, some, a certain* man ; and often approaching very near to the Indefinite Article *an, a :*

Sum welig man wæs se hæfde sumne geréfan *A rich man there was who had a reeve.*

Yet it cannot be said that an Indefinite Article had been matured in Anglosaxon. **Sum . . . sum** stands for *one . . . another* ; not *alius alium* but *alius . . . alius.* **Ða forgymdon hi þæt, and ferdon; sum to hys túne, sum to his mangunge** *Then neglected they that, and departed, one to his farm, another to his merchandise—*'*alius in villam suam, alius verò ad negotiationem suam.'*

An *one* and its negative **nán** *none.* **Wuht, wiht** *thing, creature, matter,* combined with these, makes **ánwuht, áwiht, áht** *aught* ; **nánwuht, náht** *naught, nought.*

Þing *thing* combines with sum and nán, and hence our modern *something*, *nothing*. Ne fand þær nán þing buton ealde weallas *He found there nothing but old walls.*

Man is symbolised to the sense of *one, any one,* like German man and French *on.*

Other Indefinites are : ǽlc *each,* ǽnig *any,* and its negative nǽnig *not any,* ánlépe, ǽnlýpig *single,* eall *all,* feawa *few,* manig *many* (pl. manega), óðer *other,* swilc *such,* syndrig *sundry,* þyllic *such like.*

These Indefinite Pronouns are declined as strong adjectives. But ylc which is never without the Def. Art. declines weak: se ylca, seó ylce, þæt ylce *the same.* And sylf *self* declines both strong and weak.

Indeclinable are fela *many,* Germ. viel, genoh *enough,* lyt *little,* unlyt *no little.*

§ *Some Adverbial Pronouns.*

There is a suffix variously written as hwugu, hugu, hwegu, hwega, which is of the very essence of an Indefinite, and to which it is hard to assign a value, but it is something like ' in a way,' or with a negative, ' at all.' It is found attached to hwæt, hwilc, and ǽlc, so that hwæthwegu means *something,* hwylchugu *someone,* ælcnehugu dǽl *whatever part, any part at all.*

Se is lytles geleáfan, seðe hwæthwega gelýfð and hwæthwega twynað *He is of little faith, who in a way believeth and in a way doubteth.* Þæt sǽd þe bufon ðam stǽnigan lande feól sprytte hwæthwega *The seed that upon the stony land fell sprouted somewhat.*

Hwæne (hwænne, Mark iv. 12) *sometime, some-when,* as

Hwæne **ér** we sprǽcon be **ðam** &c. *A while ago we spoke of the &c.*

Hwonlice *lightly, some little, only a little.*

Húru *at least, anyhow, for certain.* Gif ge noldon Gode libban on cildháde né on geoguðe, gecyrrað nú huru ðinga on ylde to lifes wege nu ge habbað hwonlice to swincenne *If ye would not live to God in childhood, nor in youth, turn ye now at all events in age to the way of life, now ye have little to labour in.*

The form -**inga**, -**unga**, gives a few: ánunga, áninga, ǽninga *promptly, by all means, certainly,* eallunga *altogether so.*

Three triplets in -**an**:

hér *here*	hider *hither*	heonan *hence*
þǽr *there*	þider *thither*	þonan *thence*
hwǽr *where*	hwider *whither*	hwonan *whence*

IX. THE LINK-WORD GROUP.

1. The Prepositions consist of a small number of old and a large number of new Prepositions, the latter being often made out with the adverbial termination -**an**. In the following alphabetical list the old fundamental prepositions are distinguished by CAPITALS.

The letters attached to each indicate the cases which they govern. When a small letter is used, it indicates that the case is less frequent.

abutan (A. D.) *about.*
ÆFTER (D.) *after.*
ǽr (D.) *ere.*
ÆT (D.) *at.*
andlang (G.) *along.*

bæftan (D.) *after.*
BE (D.) *about, around.*
beforan (A. D.) *before.*
begeondan (D.) *beyond.*
beheonan (D.) *on this side of.*

behindan (D.) *behind.*

beneoðan (D.) *beneath.*

betweox (D.) *among.*

betwynan (D.) *between.*

binnan (D.) *within.*

bufan (D.) *above.*

bútan (D.) *without, except.*

eác (D.) *besides.*

FOR (D. Inst. a.) *for.*

foran (D.) *in front of.*

fore (D. a.) *before, for.*

fram (D.) *from.*

gemang (A. D.) *among.*

geond (A.) *through.*

IN (A. D.) *in, into.*

innan (A. D.) *within, into.*

intó (D.) *in, into.*

MID (A. D.) *with.*

neáh (D.) *near.*

neár (D.) *nearer.*

OF (D.) *of, by.*

OFER (A. D.) *over.*

ON (A. D.) *on, in, into.*

ongeán (A. D.) *towards, against.*

on innan (D.) *within.*

on uppan (A. D.) *over, upon.*

ÓÐ (A. D.) *unto, until.*

TÓ (D.) *to.*

tó eácan (D.) *besides.*

tó emnès (D.) *alongside, abreast of.*

tó foran (D.) *before, above.*

tó geánes (A. D.) *towards, against.*

tóweard (D.) *toward.*

ÞURH (A. D.) *through, by.*

under (A. D.) *under.*

uppon (A. D.) *upon.*

WIÐ (A. D. G.) *towards, by the side of, against.*

wiðinnan (D.) *within.*

wiðútan (D.) *without.*

YMB (A.) *around, about.*

ymbútan (A.) *round about outside.*

2. The **Conjunctions** in ordinary use are as follows:—

ac *but.*

ægðer ge .. ge *both ... and.*

and *and.*

bútan *but, unless.*

eác *eke, also.*

eác swylce *likewise.*

for þam þe *forasmuch as.*

for þy *therefore.*

ge *and.*

ge ... ge *both ... and.*

gif *if.*

hwæðer...þe *whether...or.*

mid þy *since.*

náðer né .. né *neither .. nor.*

né *nor.*　　　　　　　　　　þᴀ *then, therefore.*

oððe *or.*　　　　　　　　　　þá þá *when.*

same *also.*　　　　　　　　þæt *that.*

swá . . . swá *so* . . . *as.*　　þeáh *though.*

swá same *likewise.*　　　　þeáh hwæðere *nevertheless.*

swá same swá *just as well as.*　　þonne *when, if.*

swá þeáh *however.*　　　　uton *go to, let us.*

swylce *as if.*　　　　　　　witodlice *but indeed, but*

to þon þæt *to the end that.*　　*withal.*

The preposition óð formed a conjunctive phrase óð ðæt (rarely óþ þe) often written in one word :—and hie þeáh þa ceastre aweredon oþþæt Ælfred com mid fierde *and they however defended the city until Alfred came with Fierd.* Sometimes it stood alone as a conjunction, without any pronoun : þa rád se cyning mid fierde oð he gewicode æt Baddan byrig wið Win burnan *Then rode the king with Fierd until he camped at Badbury near Wimbourne.*

As to uton, it might with equal propriety be ranked among the Interjections.

X. SYNTAX.

As there is not space for a complete description of Anglosaxon Syntax, we will attend chiefly to such structures as have anything characteristic or peculiar.

1. *Interjections.*

The Interjections serve for sudden or exclamatory beginnings of sentences : Hwæt Orpheus ðá lædde his wif mid him *Lo Orpheus then led his wife with him.*

An Interjection may be followed by a genitive of the

cause of the cry : **Wálá ðære yrmðe and wálá ðære woruldscame ðe nú habbað Engle** *Alas for the misery, and alas for the public shame that now the English have !*

After an Interjection an adjective is definite and declined weak : **Lá góda lareow** *Oh good teacher !*

2. *Verbs.*

Tense. The small number of tenses in the Anglo-saxon verb must strike the eye which is familiar with the varieties of tense-forms in the Latin verb. There is a Present and a Preterite, but no form for the Future, or the Pluperfect, or the Perfect, or Imperfect. From this poverty two consequences flow which merit attention. First, there is the make-shift use of these few, by which their power of expression was exerted to the utmost, and by which a plurality of function was laid upon single forms. Hence, an Implicit syntax, requiring vigilance in the reader. Secondly, there is the endeavour to supply by means of auxiliaries those shades of relative time which with the progress of thought or with the study of Latin came into demand. Hence an Explicit syntax, which gave the first outlines of modern English prose.

a. First then of the old forms in exerted senses. The most conspicuous is the case of the Present Tense standing for the Future (Luke xv. 18). And here the instance which claims special mention is that of **bið**, a Present of **beon** *to be.* For two reasons it claims special notice : because of its great frequency ; and because the verb *to be* having another form for the Present Tense, namely **eom eart is,** this **bið** made the more progress towards establishing itself as a distinct Future, which however it never fully achieved. Examples :

þeós biÐ geciged fæmne *This shall be called woman.*
Gif he slæpÐ, he biÐ hál *If he sleeps he will be well.*
Þu nást nú, ac þu wást syÐÐan *Thou knowest not
now, but thou shalt know hereafter*: tu nescis modo, scies
autem postea.

The Preterite discharges not only its proper function,
but also acts upon occasion for the Perfect or Pluperfect.
For the Perfect; as, **Nu smeadon gehwilce men oft,
and gyt gelóme smeagaÐ, hú se hláf þe biÐ of corne
gegearcod, and þurh fyres hætan abacen, mage
beon áwend &c.** *Now divers men have often asked and
yet do frequently ask, how the bread which is prepared from
corn and by fire's heat baked, can be changed,* &c.　For the
Pluperfect; as, **He ofslog þone aldormon þe him
lengest wunode** *He slew the alderman that had longest
dwelt with him.*

β. The more discriminative rendering of time-relations
was to be effected by means of the auxiliaries, *be, have,
may, might, shall, should, will, would.* There was yet one
more, **weorÐan**, which has since been dropped, but which
continues to hold this place in German werben. This
with the two first, *be* and *have*, are the only ones already
established as auxiliaries: the rest are but partially symbolised, and rarely appear as pure auxiliaries. The
Present **hæbbe** with the Past Participle forms a Perfect;
ic hæbbe gesæd *I have said.* The Preterite **hæfde**
in like manner goes to form a Pluperfect, as **þá hig
hæfdon hyra lof sang gesungenne** *when they had sung
their hymn.*

The Present-exact and the Imperfect are obtained by
the corresponding tenses of the verb *to be* with the Present
Participle of any verb: **nú þú þus glædlice to us**

sprecende eart *now thou art speaking to us so cheer-fully* : he mid him spræcende wæs *he was talking with him.*

Mood. The use of the Subjunctive ·Mood is well marked, but there is the less need to say much about it, as it is used just as in Latin and in the modern languages, English included. Háwa þæt se inra wind ne þe to-wende *Look well that the inner wind upset thee not.*

Modern diction has, however, been somewhat negligent of the Subjunctive, and it ˗occurs sometimes in Anglosaxon where English will not now admit it : Saga me for hwilcum þingum heofon sy gehaten heofon *Say to me on what account heaven is called heaven.*

Voice. There is no Passive Inflection. The Active verb is made to express the Passive idea. Thus, he is to lufigenne, lit. *he is to love,* signifies as much as *he is* (worthy) *to be loved.* Ælfred mec heht gewyrcean *Alfred ordered me to be made.* Hyne hét his hlaford gesyllan *His lord commanded him to be sold.* Syle hit nistigum drincan *Give it to be drunk fasting.* This is the implicit Passive.

The explicit Passive is rendered in all tenses by help-words, viz. the Present with is or byð or weorð : the Imperfect with wæs or wearð : the Perfect and Plu-perfect with is . . . geworden, and wæs . . . geworden : the Future with bið or sceal beon. Darius geseáh þæt he ofer wunnen beón wolde *Darius saw that he would be overcome.*

But these explicit Passives often labour under all the vagueness of a recently learnt lesson : and the fashion of the structure is then most idiomatic when the passive idea is conveyed by such means as the active verb affords.

Government. The most remarkable thing under this head is the great variety of verbs that take a Genitive : þa litlan cild bædon him hláfes *The little children begged for themselves bread.* He elcode his sleges *He delayed the slaying of him.* We hédað þæra crumena *We heed the crumbs.* Drihten gehelp mín *Lord help me.* Nolde ge me wæda tiðian *Ye would not grant me clothes.* Gif þu his wel notast *If thou usest it well.*

Many verbs take a genitive sometimes and not always. An important verb that is constant in this government is unnan, one of the Præt.-Præs.—and ic ge an minum fæder Æþelræde cynge þæs landes æt Norþtúne . and þæs seolfer hiltan swyrdes ðe Ulfeytel ahte . and þære byrnan þe mid Morcere is . and þæs horses ðe þurbrand me geaf . and þæs hwitan horses þe Leofwine me geaf. *And I grant to my father king Æthelred the land at Norton, and the silver-hilted sword that Ulfcytel owned, and the byrnie that is with Morcer, and the horse that Thurbrand gave me, and the white horse that Leofwine gave me.*

3. *Substantives.*

Flat construction. Substantives construe with Substantives in a manner which, though we have not lost, yet nevertheless sometimes causes us a surprise. Thus, woruld men *worldly men*:—and fela oðre unþeáwas ðe woruld men to nanum láðe ne taliað *and many other bad habits which worldly men account no harm of.*

Flectional. An important feature is the frequency of the Qualificatory Genitive :—se scires man Leofric *the shire-man Leofric ;* geméenes hádes preost *a priest*

of inferior grade ; se Godes wer *the man of God*;
dæges leoht *day-light*; wífhádes man *a female person.*

4. *Adjectives.*

The distinction between the Strong and Weak forms
of the Adjective is one which, though delicate and subtle,
is neither vague nor fanciful, but real and firmly defined.
Which of the two forms shall be used depends entirely
upon the logical relation of the Adjective to the other
words of the sentence. The distinction is one of thought,
and, when it has been once apprehended, the student
will require no definitions. For an outward rule the following may be sufficiently near : the Weak form is used
when it is preceded by a genitive, or an adjective, or a
pronoun, or an article, or an interjection ; but it would be
too much to say that in all other cases the Strong form
is used. The Weak is in fact a Definite and the Strong
an Indefinite form, and in some grammars the terms Definite and Indefinite are employed, when adjectives are
spoken of, instead of Strong and Weak.

The Syntax of the Comparative Adjective offers a fine
illustration of this principle, for as it is in its nature a
definite adjective, so it is employed only in the Weak
declension. The Ordinal Numerals exemplify the same
principle, being highly definite in thought, and Weak in
form.

Comparison. The particle of Comparison answering
to our *than* is þonne; Hwæt is fúlre þonne meox ;
and swa ðeah, gif þu his wel notast, hwæt bið
wæstmbærre ? *What is fouler than dung ? and yet, if
thou makest good use of it, what is more fruitful ?*

Þonne applies only to Uneven Comparison, that is,

where one side of the Comparison is in excess or defect of the other. In Even Comparison the formula is **swá**
. . . **swá :—Nán gereord is swá healic swá Ebreisc** *No language is so elevated as Hebrew.*

Another sort of Comparison, which may be called the Comparison of Double Ratio, is expressed by a repeated **swa** with a pair of Comparatives :—**And swá neár ende þissere worulde swá máre ehtnys þæs deofles** *And the nearer* (it is to the) *end of the world, the more the devil's ferocity.*

5. Adverbs.

Adverbs are formed from Adjectives, in the Positive by the termination -**e**; in the Comparative and Superlative degrees the Strong Adjectives stand unaltered in -**or** and -**ost**. See examples above, vii. 3.

The genitival termination is much used as an adverbial inflection, and it survives in modern English, in that -*s* which often closes our adverbs. Thus **norðweardes** *northwards*, **þiderweardes** *thitherwards*, **hamweardes** *homewards*. **Lǽt hit standan geárlanges** *Let it stand for a year.*

Ða cwæð heó ðæt heó ne mihte hyre dæles né he his *Then said she that she could not* (*do it*) *on her part nor he on his.*

The genitival adverbs are not necessarily of the same form as the genitive of the declension to which the substantive belongs. For instance, the true genitive of **niht** *night* is **nihte**, but the genitival adverb is **nihtes** *by night*, just as in German they say 𝔑𝔞𝔠𝔥𝔱𝔰, which is not the substantival genitive of 𝔑𝔞𝔠𝔥𝔱.

Fóron án streces dæges and nihtes *They marched at one stretch day and night.*

6. *Numerals.*

Cardinal Numeration. In the collocation of the
numeral grades, that precedency of the ·units, which is
now to us a picturesque archaism, is in Anglosaxon the
rule. Thus **six and fíftig** *six and fifty*: **seofon and
feówertig** *seven and forty.*

But when there are hundreds in the sum, these generally stand first, taking also the substantive with them:
**Hundteóntig wintra and seofon and feówertig win-
tra** *A hundred winters and seven and forty winters.*

And here observe, that the Cardinals are sometimes
construed as substantives, and sometimes as adjectives.
Speaking roughly, the higher numbers incline to be
substantival and to govern genitives; the lower to be
adjectival and stand in concord with their substantives.
Þreó hund manna and eahtatýne men *Three hundred
of men and eighteen men.* **Twelf hund hída** *Twelve
hundred (of) hides.* **Binnan þrittigum nihtum** *Within
thirty nights.*

Ordinal Numeration. When, in Ordinal numeration,
units are added to tens, the units retain the Cardinal form
if they come first; but if they are stated after the tens,
then they become subject to the Ordinal inflection. This
is the more interesting to us because the distinction is
still in use.

Án and twéntigoðe *one and twentieth.*

Fíf and twéntigoðe *five and twentieth.*

Þý twéntigoðan dæge and þý feórþan Septembris
The twenty and fourth day of September.

The Ordinals come into play where 'half' is added in
English to a Cardinal number. So in German **anbertþalb**

one and a half, þrittþalb *two and a half.* He ricsode nigonteóðe healf geár *He reigned eighteen years and a half.* Se bát wæs geworht of þriddan healfre hýde *The boat was made of two and a half hides.*

7. *Pronouns Personal, Reflexive, Possessive.*

A well-marked idiom of Gothic syntax is that by which the predicate of a person is rendered by a neuter pronoun. Ic hyt eom *I it am,* where we now say *It is I,* or *I am he.* This formula still exists in German Ich bin es.

In the First and Second Persons there is no distinct form for the Reflexive Pronoun, but the simple Personal Pronoun is used reflexively: **Ic me reste** *I rest myself.* **Begyrd þe and sceo þe** *Gird thyself and shoe thyself.* Neither is there any Reflexive pronoun of the Third Person answering to the Latin *se, sui, sibi,* which modern English expresses by *himself, herself, itself, themselves.* There once existed such a pronoun, and a trace of it survives in the poetic diction; but it had died out before the historic period of the language. The practice here is the same as in the First and Second Persons. It is simply to use **he, heó, hit,** as a Reflexive Pronoun. Thus :—

Petrus stód and wyrmde hine *Peter stood and warmed himself.*

Ða ongan se Fariseisca on him smeagan *Then began the Pharisee to think within himself.*

But the modern formula was already in use. Where antithesis or emphasis required it, or where in translation it was suggested by the original, **sylf** was added, as **Oðre he hále gedyde, hine sylfne he ne mæg hálne gedón**

He healed others, himself he cannot make whole ; seipsum
non potest salvum facere [1].

Possessive. This is at first but the Genitive of the
three Personal Pronouns, min, þin, his, hire. Gif ðæt
land ðín is, se rén is mín *If the land is thine, the rain
is mine.*

The Possessive pronoun sometimes takes the addition
of ágen *own*, just as at present : Ða cóm Æðelred
cyning hám to his ágenre ðeode *Then came king
Æthelred home to his own people.*

The Reciprocal pronoun which we now render by
such formulæ as *each other, one another*, is expressed in
Anglosaxon by a repetition of the Personal pronoun :
And hí æt þære byrig hí gemetton *And they met each
other at the city* : Hí hí gedǽldon *They separated from one
another.*

8. *Pronouns Demonstrative* (Definite Article) *and Relative.*

The Demonstrative þæt is joined in the Singular
number with the Plural sind, to express *namely, such are* :
Twá wiðerrǽde ðing ðeodde Drihten on ðisum
cwyde, þæt sind, ymbh'dignyssa and lustas *Two
contradictory things the Lord associated in this sentence,
namely anxieties and pleasures.*

---

[1] In modern English for greater distinctness we habitually form
the Reflexive pronoun by the addition of *self, selves* ; but still we are
familiar to this day with the reflex use of *me, thee, him, her, them,* as
poetic and archaic.   So in the Psalter; 'I will lay me down in
peace'—'they get them away together, and lay them down in their
dens.'

    'The shepherd shifts his mantle's fold,
      And wraps him closer from the cold.'—*Marmion.*

Out of the Demonstrative Pronoun **se, seo, þæt**, the Definite Article was formed. The manner of its application differs from that of the modern language, both in regard to its presence and its absence. It is sometimes employed where we should now omit it, but much more is it absent where we should use it. The most striking instance of its introduction where to us it appears to be only in the way, is where it is put between a possessive pronoun and its substantive. (Matt. xviii. 35.)

It is absent where we now use it before titles, before national designations, and before river-names : **Ælfred cyning oft gefeaht wið Denum** *Alfred* the *king often fought with* the *Danes.*

Gebete swa biscop him tæce *Let him make amends as* the *bishop shall direct him.* Many like instances occur, as might be expected in a language in which the Definite Article was yet in its earlier stage. A most interesting contrast to our present usage is its absence from river-names : **behionan Humbre** *on this side of* the *Humber*, **begeondan Humbre** *on that side of* the *Humber.* **Andlang Temese, þæt up on Ligean, andlang Ligean óð hire ǽ wylm, þanon . . . up on Usan óð Watlinga stræt** *Along* the *Thames, and so up on* the *Lea, along the Lea, up to her fountain-head, thence . . . up on* the *Ouse to Watling Street*[1].

Relative. When the Relative pronoun is required to stand in an oblique Case, there is no single word in Anglosaxon that can fulfil the function, like our modern

---

[1] There is not an instance in the English Bible (1611) of a river-name with Def. Art. :—it is always Jordan, Euphrates, never 'the Jordan.' This feature of the modern language first enters Bible English in the New Testament Revision of 1881.

F

whose and *whom.* For these words were at that time only used as Interrogatives and Indefinites.

This difficulty sprang from the fact that the Relative pronoun þe was indeclinable[1]. The remedy was to add to þe, either next to it or after intervening words, a Personal pronoun carrying the requisite Case; as **þe þurh hine** *through whom,* **þe þurh his** *through whose,* **se wæs Karles sunu þe Æþelwulf West Seaxna cyning his dohtor hæfde him to cuene** *He was son of (that) Charles whose daughter Æthelwulf King of Wessex had to queen.*

To express *whereon, on which,* it was necessary to subjoin **on** in like manner: **and ic ge ann Eadrice Wynflæde suna þæs swyrdes þe seó hand ys on gemearcod** *And I grant to Eadric the son of Wynflæd the sword on which the hand is marked.*

9. *Pronouns Interrogative and Indefinite.*

Just as they said **Ic hit eom** (above, § 7), so also they said interrogatively **Hwæt eart þu?** for *Who art thou?*

The Indefinite Pronoun **man (mon)** supplies the convenient function of a Personal Pronoun Impersonal, and it often comes into action where we now use a Passive verb: **ðá wæs sionoðlic ġemót on þære mæran stowe ðe mon hateð Clofeshoas** *then was there a synodical assembly in the celebrated place which is called Clovesho.*

10. *Pronoun Adverb.*

Under this head the most important matter is the instrument of Negation. This, in its simplest form, is **ne** preceding the verb.

[1] The same inability showed itself in the Hebrew language: it rose from the same cause and was met in the same manner.

Þæs ne eom ic wyrðe *I am not worthy of that.*

Ne wyrn þu hym *Deny thou him not.*

When the negation has to be strengthened, another and secondary negative is placed after the verb: there is no fastidiousness about a double negative, any more than there is in Plato and all the best Greek writers.

ne fengon nan þing *They caught nothing.* Nán þæra þe þár sæt ne dorste hine acsian hwæt he wære *None of those that there sate durst ask him who he was.* Ne heora nán geréfscipe oððe mangunge ne drífe *Let no one of them pursue the trade of reeve or dealer.*

11. *Prepositions.*

1. **Government.** The government of the several prepositions has been indicated above, and there is not much to add. Let us choose one for exemplification. The cases taken by wið are three; and the corresponding shades of meaning are generally manifest:

ACCUSATIVE. Ða tyn leorning cnihtas gebulgon wið ða twegen gebróðru *The ten disciples were angry with* (against) *the two brothers.*

Wið þone garsecg *By the ocean.*

Sæton wið þone weg *They sate by* (facing) *the way.*

And þæs on Eastron worhte Ælfred cyning, lytle werode, geweorc. æt Æþelinga eigge, and of þam geweorc was winnende wiþ þone here *And the ensuing Easter wrought king Alfred with a little band a Work at Athelney, and from the Work was fighting against the* (heathen) *host.*

Sý he fáh wið. ðone cyng and wið ealle his freond *Be he foe to* (against) *the king and to* (against) *all friends of his.*

Dative. We willað wið ðam golde grið fæstnian *We are willing in consideration of the gold to establish peace.*

Fæder gesealde bearn wið weorðe *The father sold the child for a price.*

Læcedomas wið eallum untrumnyssum heafdes *Prescriptions for all infirmities of head.* Læcedomas wið eallum tiedernessum eagena *Prescriptions for all affections of the eyes.*

Genitive. Ða he forð on þæt leóht com, þa beseah he hine under bæc wið þæs wifes *As he came forth to the light, he looked round him behind towards the woman.*

Hafoc wið ðæs holtes *Hawk towards the holt.*

Þá wende he hine west wið Exanceastres *Then turned he him west towards Exeter.*

2. **Function.** Prepositions live by usage merely. They are so far removed from the etymological pedigree of their origin, that their offices are held by tradition only, and having no acknowledged mooring in reason, they do from time to time shift function. The variation of prepositional function is curious and instructive ; moreover it offers one of the firmest characteristics for distinguishing the several periods of the English language.

A rudimentary scheme of Prepositional functions may be sketched by pairing off the contraries :

in	out *adv.*
on	of
to	from
at	by

It is clear that these pairs are formed of contradictories : it being remembered that ' by ' means ' somewhere round about,' and therefore not ' at.' It is further clear that there is a community of sentiment in each column which unites it within itself, and which sets it as a whole in contradiction to the other column as a whole.

And it is no more than natural that a solidarity should arise between the members of either column so that they should be able to step up or down along the vertical line and fill a neighbour's office. And as a consequence of this facility, no great inconvenience would result from the retirement partial or complete of any of these prepositions, seeing that not one of them is indispensably necessary to the action of the language.

OUT, OF, FROM, BY. It does not appear that út *out* was a preposition by itself, but with the preposition **of** it acted as an adverbial support: **gangan út of earce** *to go out of the ark.*

Of obtained great prevalence, being, among other things, the preposition of passivity, a function which in the earlier time it shared with **fram**, but at length took altogether to itself.

The preposition **be,** which in Anglosaxon signified *round about, concerning,* came at length in the form *by* to be the companion of the passive verb, having superseded **of** in that function.

IN, ON, TO, AT. In the elder Anglosaxon writings we find **in,** but it fell out of common use, leaving behind it a feeble descendant **innan.** Its chief functions passed to its subaltern **on,** which became one of the very greatest prepositions in Anglosaxon. **Nis nán witega butan weorþscipe, buton on his éðele, and on his mǽgþe, and on his húse** *No prophet is without honour, except in his native country, and in his tribe; and in his house.* This preposition holds in Anglosaxon a breadth of area almost comparable with that of *of* in modern English.

Many a place where we now use *of* was indeed filled by
on : cyning on Engla lande *king of England,* **biscop
on Lundene** *bishop of London.*

The distinction between *on* and *to* is sensibly de-
monstrated in a place where we, after the original, read
a ring on his hand and shoes on his feet. The Anglosaxon
has **hring on his hand, and gescý to his fótum.**

But it is with *at* more especially that *to* comes into
competition. In Anglosaxon we find **to** where now *at*
is preferred, quite often enough to modify our wonder
at the great prevalence of *to* in Devonshire. Such a
phrase as this, **wæs Hama swán geréfa to Súðtúne**
Hama was herd-reeve at Sutton, is of constant occurrence
in Devonshire [1].

But **æt** prevailed in connection with names of places,
and we find it in Anglosaxon both (1) where we still use *at,*
and also (2) where, in the subservience of the place-name
to the purpose of personal description, we have now sub-
stituted *of.* Besides this, (3) **æt** has a very peculiar use in
Anglosaxon, of which we have not a trace remaining. We
can say ' at a time ' and ' at a place,' but not ' at a person.'
But as Latin says ' apud eum ' so Anglosaxon **æt him**
(John x. 18). The following quotation illustrates all these
uses of **æt : Her swutelað on ðissum gewrite ðæt
Eþelstan bisceop gebohte æt Leofrice æt Blace-
wellon fif hide landes æt Intebyrga** *Here appears in
this writing that bishop Ethelstan bought* of *Leofric* of
Blackwell five hides of land at Inkberrow. **Hit gelamp
ðæt hire fæder aborgude xxx punda æt Godan**

---

[1] Not so very many years ago, schoolmasters in Devonshire were
wont to tell how that Atterbury gave as a reason for unwillingness
to go into Devonshire, that the natives could not pronounce *at,* and
he had no fancy to be called *To-terbury !*

It happened that her father borrowed thirty pounds of Goda [1].

It also has uses that are familiar to us : **He cnucode æt þære dura** *He knocked at the door.* Also Mark iv. 1.

12. *Conjunctions.*

Ðá ðá (literally *then then*) expresses *when*, and a third ðá in a subsequent clause expresses a responsive *then* : **Ðá ðá se forma cýðere gestæned wæs, Saulus heóld ealra ðæra stænendra hacelan** *When the first martyr was stoned, Saul held the coats of all the stoners.* These two particles may be separated by an intervening word : **Ðá he ðá ðás andsware onfeng, ðá ongann he sóna singan** *When he had received this answer, then he began forthwith to sing.*

Distinguish **ne** *neither*, *nor*, the conjunction, from **ne** the particle of simple negation. The latter had a short vowel, while the former was probably **né**. In our quotations it shall be so marked for distinction sake.

Ne slæpð né ne hnappað se ðe hylt Israhel, lit. *Not sleepeth nor not slumbereth he who keepeth Israel.*

Behealdað heofenan fuglas, forþam þe hig ne sáwað, né hig ne ripað, né hig ne gadriaþ on berne *Behold heaven's fowls, for they sow not, nor do they reap, nor gather into barn.*

Ge wénað þæt ge nán gecyndelic gód né gesælþe on innan eów selfum næbben *Ye ween that ye have no natural good nor happiness within yourselves.*

The simple negative **ne** coalesces with some verbs, as

---

[1] This use of *at* lived on to the 14th and even into the 16th century. Wiclif, A.D. 1388:—ȝe schulen haue no meede at ȝour fadir. Matt. vi. 1. The original English Psalter (1539):—The lyons roaring after theyr praye to seke theyr meate at God. Ps. civ. 21.

here **næbben** for **ne hæbben** ; but this never happens to the conjunction **né**.

The most ordinary formula for the subjunction of sentence to sentence is **þæt** *that,* as in modern English. See the preceding quotation.

The conjunction **swilce** *as if* is generally followed by a verb in the Subjunctive Mood :—**Þuhte him swilce hit swefen wære** *It seemed to him as if it were a dream.* **Þu húwast swilce þu ðinum cildum hit sparige** *Thou pretendest as if thou be saving it for thy children.* Also without verb : **Martha swanc ða swilce on rewette, and Maria sæt stille swilce æt ðære hyðe** *Martha toiled there as if at rowing, and Mary sate still as if at the hythe.*

For coupling words in pairs (especially opposites) **ge** is used :—**ealde ge geonge** *old and young* ; **leófum ge láðum** *to friends and foes* ; **feor ge neah** *far and near* ; **cwucra ge deadra** *of quick and dead.*

For clustering words or phrases the formula is **ge . . . ge,** *both. . . . and, as well . . . as.* Thus **ge wið cyning ge wið ealdorman ge wið geréfan** *alike against king and against ealdorman and against sheriff.*

Sometimes **ægðer** precedes : **ægðer ge godcundra háda ge woruldcundra** *both of spiritual and temporal orders* : **and hu him ðá speów ægðer ge mid wige ge mid wisdome** *and how success attended them both in war and in counsel.*

The formula of alternation is **hwæðer . . . þe . . . þe** : —**on þam múðe we habbað swæcc, and tocnáwað hwæþer hit bið þe wered þe biter þæt we ðicgað** *In the mouth we have Taste, and distinguish whether it is sweet or bitter what we eat.*

XI. DERIVATIVES AND COMPOUNDS.

Two chief means there are for the supply of new words, namely Derivation and Compound-making. We must distinguish between Derivatives and Compounds. In the Derivative the first part is principal and the second part is accessory; but in the Compound this is reversed. Thus æðeling *prince* is a Derivative; and the object of thought is contained in the first part æðel *inheritance, estate*, with reference to which the second part ing serves as a formative of the word and a definer of the expression. But brim fugol *sea-fowl* is a Compound; and here the second part is principal in thought, while the first part is subservient and qualifying.

1. **Derivatives.** Substantives are formed with the terminations—

-a; thus from múð *mouth*, múða *estuary*; from gild *guild*, gilda *guild-brother*.

-ere; for the agent, bacere *baker*, bócere *scribe*.

-en; to form feminines, munec *monk*, mynecen *nun*; wealh *male-slave*, wylen *female-slave*; god *god*, gyden *goddess*. In these the root-vowel suffers Umlaut.

-t and -ð form abstracts, bærnet *burning*, treowð *troth*, geoguð *youth*.

-ung; feminine abstracts to verbs in -ian, gelaðung *invitation*, from gelaðian *to invite*, stǽnung *stoning*, from stǽnan *to stone*.

-nes, -nis; also fem. abstracts; brádnis, langnis, heahnis, deopnis *breadth, length, height, depth*.

-ing forms an adjectival word signifying a relation, such as we should now express by 'of the'; Sceafing *the man of the sheaf*, æðeling *he of the* æðel; and this

form became great as a patronymic, **Ælfred Æþelwulfing**
Alfred (son) of Æthelwulf.

Adjectives are formed with the terminations—

-en ; from **stán** *stone,* **sténen** *of stone* ; with umlaut.

-ig ; from **hungor** *hunger,* **hungrig** *hungry.*

-iht ; from **stán** *stone,* **stániht** *stony.*

-isc ; from **ceorl** *commoner,* **cyrlisc** ; with umlaut.

-ol (-el) ; from **wacan** *to wake,* **wacol** *vigilant.*

2. **Compounds.** Among the oldest are those in which
a Particle is prefixed to a substantive or adjective, as
bi spel *parable,* **bi word** *proverb,* **for wyrd** *ruin,* **ge scy**
pair of shoes, **ge limp** *chance,* **ofer mód** *pride,* **or sorh**
tranquil, **un gelimp** *misfortune,* **un lust** *evil passion,*
un þeaw *vice,* **under cyning** *under-king,* **up flor** *upper
floor,* **up land** *high lying land,* **ymbe hwyrft** *circum-
ference.*

Particular attention is due to a certain collective value
of the prefix **ge-** as in **sceó** *shoe,* **ge scy** *a pair of shoes* or
shoes generally; **sculdor** *shoulder,* **ge scyldre** *the shoulders*;
timber *building material,* **ge timbre** *an edifice*; **wéd**
garment, **ge wéde** *vesture, robes*; **botl** *shelter,* **ge bytle**
range of buildings. This is worthy of particular notice,
not only for its area in Anglosaxon as for its large
sphere in the other Teutonic languages, especially in
German.

Compounds are also formed by the union of a particle
with a verb; of a noun with a noun; of a noun with
a verb; of adverbs, pronouns, prepositions with one another. It is by these new combinations that the functions
of language are replenished with new verbs, new substantives, new adjectives, new adverbs, new pronouns, new
prepositions, new conjunctions, new interjections.

New Verbs are formed by composition with adverbs and adverbial particles: á German er-; æt *at*; be *about, near, by*: ed *again, over again* (Latin *re-*); efen *even*; for German ver- produces strong effects; ful *fully*; forð *forth*; ge, not always the effete prefix, but having sometimes an important effect on the sense; mis expressing disturbance; of sometimes expressing attainment of aim; on *on, in*; óð German ent-; to indicates division like Latin *dis-* and German ʒer-; under *under*; wið *against*. By composition with these particles verbs acquire new powers, sometimes transcending the sum of the parts.

á hebban *exalt*	*from*	hebban *heave*
æt berstan *break away*	„	berstan *burst*
be gán *cultivate, exercise*	„	gán *go*
be cuman *arrive*	„	cuman *come*
ed lǽcan *repeat*	„	lǽcan *play*
efen lǽcan *imitate*	„	lǽcan *play*
for gifan *concede, forgive*	„	gifan *give*
ful fremman *accomplish*	„	fremman *promote*
forð faran *depart*	„	faran *fare*
ge winnan *conquer, win*	„	winnan *fight*
mis endebyrdian *mal-officiate*	„	endebyrdian *order duly*
of rídan *capture*	„	rídan *ride*
on fón *receive*	„	fón *take*
óð fleón *escape*	„	fleón *flee*
tó cnáwan *distinguish*	„	cnáwan *know*
under standan *understand*	„	standan *stand*
wið sacan *dispute*	„	sacan *contend*

The sense-effects of these verbal prefixes are often very fine, and sometimes subtle. The beginner should not overlook the difference between beran and áberan, between **cuman** and **ácuman**. Still less that between **cuman** and **becuman**, which signifies attainment of object, in a manner approaching the German befommen. In the history of Nebuchadnezzar it represents the Latin *pervenire*, and can hardly be rendered in English but by 'recover' and 'return':—**ic becom to wurðmynte mines cynerices and min mennisce hiw me becom** *I recovered my royal dignity and my human form returned to me* [1].

for- is a powerful prefix; **Micel gesælð bið ðe, ðæt ðu on ðínre gesælðe ne forfare** *Great luck will it be to thee, that thou in thy luck come not to grief.*

ge- is so largely an effete and idle prefix, that we may easily overlook cases in which it has a vigorous effect; as before verbs of going, **gán, faran, rídan,** &c. it makes the compound mean 'to get by going, marching, riding':—**þæt we scylon eac on ealre clænnesse healdan, gif we aht gefaran scylon** *which we must also with all purity preserve, if we are to succeed in getting anything.* Analogously **ascian** *to ask* but **geascian** *learn, get informed.*

to- has strong effects; **hi becómon to ðam ísenan geate and ðæt tosprang þærrihte him togeanes** *they arrived at the iron gate and it sprang open thereright before them.* **Ðæt deofolgild þe þu ær wurðodest to bræc** *The idol which thou formerly worshippedst brake in pieces* [2].

New Substantives grow out of the drawing together of two old Substantives.

---

[1] The history of this word is the more interesting because of its great place in modern English, where it has superseded **weorðan.**

[2] Compare Judges ix. 53 in the Bible of 1611.

æppel treó *appletree* *from* æppel *apple and* treó *tree*
bur þegn *chamberlain* „ búr *chamber* „ þegn *servant*
ciric sang *church-singing* „ cirice *church* „ sang *song*
dǽd bót *penance* „ dǽd *deed* „ bót *bettering*
disc þegn *dish-thane* „ disc *dish* „ þegn *thane*
earm hring *bracelet* „ earm *arm* „ hring *ring*
fót ádl *gout* „ fót *foot* „ ádl *disease*
grǽs hoppa *grasshopper* „ grǽs *grass* „ hoppa *hopper*
hancrǽd *cockcrowing* „ hana *cock* „ crǽd *crowing*
hand geweorc *handiwork* „ hand *hand* „ geweorc *work*
inwit searo *machination* „ inwit *guile* „ searo *device*
land sǽta *squatter* „ land *land* „ sǽta *settler*
man cild *boy* „ man *man* „ cild *child*
mán áð *perjury* „ mán *crime* „ áð *oath*
nýd þearf *necessity* „ nýd *need* „ þearf *want*
níð hete *rancour* „ níð *spite* „ hete *hate*
rím cræft *arithmetic* „ rím *number* „ cræft *craft*

sand geweorp *sand-bank* „ sand *sand* „ { geweorp *casting up*

setel gang *sun-set* „ setel *rest* „ gang *going*
treów wyrhta *carpenter* „ treów *tree* „ wyrhta *wright*
uht sang *prime* (matins) „ uhte *dawn* „ sang *song*
wín berige *grape* „ wín *wine* „ berige *berry*
yð hengest *ship* „ yð *wave* „ hengest *horse*

Some of this class have greatly changed their character by the throwing back of the tone on the first part and the extreme generalisation of the sense of the second part. By this transfer the relations of the two parts have been inverted, and the compounds hav become very like Derivatives. Such are **cristen dóm** *Christianity*, **cild hád** *childhood*, **hlaford scipe** *lordship*, **hiw rǽden** *family*.

New Adjectives are formed thus: fýr heard *hardened by fire*, from fýr *fire* and heard *hard*; lof georn *greedy of praise*, from lof *praise* and georn *eager*; meolc liðe *soft as milk* from meolc *milk* and liðe *mild*.

But here again, as in the substantives, a few adjectives, from frequently standing in the second place, have come to be mere formatives, and some of them have lost their independent existence.

Such are fæst *fast*, full *full*, leás *devoid of*, líc *like*, sum *same*. The two latter only in compounds. Examples: árfæst *honorable*, geleáfful *faithful*, árleás *dishonorable*, gástlic *ghostly*, wynsum *winsome*.

New Adverbs are obtained by composition. Thus in place of the old adverb soð, as soð ic secge eow *truly I say unto you*, came the compound soð lice, and this pattern of the compound with -lice was followed by a whole troop of new adverbs, insomuch that it has become the chief adverbial model of the English language. This -lice -*ly*, from frequently filling this office, became at length a mere adverbial formative. Similar was the lot of the words weard, riht (rihte), lang, much used to form compound adverbs of Place, thus—niðerweard *netherward*, hiderweard *hitherward*, hamweardes *homewards*, wherein weard adds nothing to the matter, but only gives point or explicitness. So with the expressions eástrihte and eástlang *eastwardly*, and þær rihte *thereright*.

New Pronouns are swilc from swá and lic, literally *so-like*, whence our *such*: also þæs lic *this-like*, and hwilc from hwý and lic, *what-like*, whence our *which*. From nán *none* and wuht, wiht *whit* was formed nanwuht, náwiht, *nothing*, whence our *nought* and *not*.

New Prepositions and **Conjunctions** may be seen above in the lists of these parts of speech.

New Interjections are eá lá from eá and lá : from wá and lá was formed wá lá wá, which became *well-a-way, well-a-day*.

XII. PROSODY.

Although this little book was destined only to supply the most elementary guidance in the reading of Anglo-saxon Prose, yet it will hardly seem complete without a few words upon the mechanism of the Poetry. This poetical mechanism is so simple and so ingenious, effecting so much by means so small, contrasting moreover so strongly with all our modern notions of poetical frame-work, that it is decidedly one of the attractions of the mother-tongue, enlisting the curiosity of the student, and beguiling his path till the first difficulties are surmounted.

The chime of the verse is produced by words with like initials, and this is called Alliteration, or Letter-play. The lines are short, and run in pairs, being coupled together by the alliteration. In a typical example the first member of each couplet has the alliterative letter twice, and the second member has it once. To illustrate this and other features it will be convenient to have a specimen before us. The beautiful fragment of 'The Ruined City' shall furnish a sample :—

1	hryre wong gecrong,	the crash cracked the pavement
2	gebrocen to beorgum;	broken into barrows :
3	þær iu beorn monig	where once many a baron
4	glædmod and gold-beorht	glad - hearted and gold-bright

5	gleoma ge frætwed	in gleaming array,
6	wlonc and wingal	wanton and wine-hot
7	wig hyrstum scán ;	in war-harness shone :
8	seah on sinc on sylfor	saw treasures of silver
9	on searo gimmas :	with settings of gems—
10	on eád on æht	and stock and store
11	on eorcan stan :	· and precious stone—
12	on þás beorhtan burg	saw this bright burgh
13	bradan rices.	of broad dominion.

In considering this specimen, let us begin, not from the top, but from the last lines. Lines 12 + 13 are a couplet, with B twice in 12 and once in 13. So of 2 + 3. In 6 + 7 the alliterative letter is W, and its distribution is the same. In 4 + 5 the letter is G; and it seems to occur four times, twice in each member. But this is not really the case; the G of ge-, a toneless prefix, does not count. So completely does this rule hold, that the initial of such a prefix can neither bear part in the alliteration, nor prevent the letter which follows it from acting as an initial. The following from *Beowulf* illustrates this in each couplet. In the first couplet G is the alliterative letter, and it is initial in **for gyldan**. In the second couplet W is the letter, and it is initial in **ge worhte**.

Grendle for gyldan	to Grendel make good
gúð ræsa fela	grapples many—
ðára þe he ge worhte	those that he wrought
tó West Denum.	upon the West-Danes.

This leads us to the important observation that only the / high-pitched words can carry the Alliteration.

Returning now to our first specimen, we observe that 8 + 9 is abnormal in having the alliterative letter thrice in the first member. But perhaps the superior tonic elevation of **sinc** and **sylfor** over **seah**, reduces the initial sound of the latter to insignificance. In 10+11 the alliteration is vocalic. And here observe that the vowels are all different. To our inexact and uncultivated notions about vowels they might seem hardly distinct, and little better than three E's. But they are in fact three different vowels, viz. eá, éo, and eo. Note this :—In vocalic alliteration not identity of vowels, but diversity, was aimed at. Thus—

Eotenas and ylfe	Giants and elves
and orceas	and hobgoblins.

A still more subtle feature is this :—The sense does not seek to run with the alliteration, but rather alternates with it. The lines from 2 to 13 pair off in alliterative couples : but line 1 belongs to a previous alliterative couple, so that the quotation is abrupt as regards the alliteration, though complete as regards the sense. As regards the sense we should couple the lines thus—1 + 2, 3 + 4, &c. But in regard to the alliteration they couple as follows—2 + 3, 4 + 5, &c. So the grammatical and the poetic articulations overlap one another, and produce a linked chain, not indeed running with machine-like regularity, but shewing here and there by glimpses, so that the keen observer may catch the latent ideal.

POSTSCRIPT to x. 2.

In the Syntax of the Verb a point has been omitted which ought to be included in any such sketch, however brief. There are many cases in which Modern English uses a Participle but Anglosaxon an Infinitive. For the present purpose one example may suffice, as in Matt. xx. 3, **he geseah óðre standan** *he saw others standing*. This is a characteristic of the old language as compared with the new.

SOME PASSAGES

FROM THE

ANGLOSAXON GOSPELS.

From Thorpe's edition, London, 1842. His accents are kept, which no doubt reflect his manuscript faithfully. But the hyphens, which are an artificial addition, I have removed. The translation is from the Latin. The language belongs to the best period ; but the manuscripts are rather late, and the orthography is a little depraved. This decadence is chiefly observable in the confusion of the vowels i and y. See p. 7.

St. Matth. v. 37–42.

Soðlice sy eower spræc, Hyt ys, hyt ys; Hyt   1
nys, hyt nys; soðlice gyf þar mare byð, þæt byð   2
of yfele. Ge gehyrdon þæt gecweden wæs, Eage   3
for eage, and toð for toð: soðlice ic secge eow,   4
Ne winne ge ongen þa ðe eow yfel doð: and gyf   5
hwa slea þe on þin swyþre wenge, gegearwa hym   6
þæt oðer. And þam ðe wyle on dome wið þe   7
flitan, and niman þine tunecan, læt him to þinne   8
wæfels. And swa hwa swa þe genyt þusend stapa,   9
gá mid him oðre twa þusend. Syle þam ðe þe   10
bidde, and þam þe wylle æt þé borgian, ne wyrn   11
þu hym.   12

St. Matth. x. 5–13.

Ðas twelf se Hælend sende, hym bebeodende, and   13
cweþende : Ne fare ge on þeoda weg, and ne ga ge   14
innan Samaritana ceastre: ac gað má to þam   15

sceapum þe forwurdon Israhela hiw rædene. Se 16
Hælend cwæþ to hys leorning cnyhtum : Gað and 17
bodiað, cweþende, Ðæt heofena rice genealæcþ. 18
Hælað untrume, aweccead deade, clænsiað hreofle, 19
drifað út deoflu : ge onfengon to gyfe, syllað 20
to gyfe. Næbbe ge gold, ne seolfer, ne feoh 21
on eowrum bigyrdlum; ne codd on wege, ne twa 22
tunecan, né gescý, ne gyrde : soþlice se wyrhta ys 23
wyrþe hys metes. On swa hwylce burh oððe 24
ceastre swa ge in gað, acsiað hwa sy wyrþe on 25
þære; and wuniað þær oþ ge út gan. Ðonne ge 26
in gan soþlice on þæt hus, gretað hit, cweþende, 27
Sy syb þysum huse. And gyf þæt hus witodlice 28
wyrþe byð, eower syb cymþ ofer hyt: gyf hyt 29
soþlice wyrþe ne byð, eower syb byþ to eow 30
gecyrred.   31

St. Matth. xviii. 23-35.

Dys sceal on ðære xxiii. wucan ofer Pentecosten.

Forþam is heofena ríce ánlic þam cyninge þe hys
þeowas geradegode.   24. And þa he þæt geråd sette, hym
wæs án broht se hym sceolde tyn þusend punda. 25. And
þa he næfde hwanon he hyt agulde, hyne het hys hlaford
gesyllan, and hys wíf and hys cild, and eall þæt he ahte.
26. Ða astrehte se þeow hyne, and cwæð : Hlaford, hafa
geþyld on me, and ic hyt þe eall agylde.   27. Ða gemiltsode se hlaford hym, and forgeaf hym þone gylt.   28. Ða
se þeowa út eode, hê gemétte hys efen þeowan se hym
sceolde án hund penega : and he nam hyne þa, and
forþrysmode hyne, and cwæð: Agif þæt þu me scealt.
29. And þa astrehte hys efen þeowa hyne, and bæd hyne,
and þus cwæð : Geþyldega, and ic hyt þe eall agife.

30. He þa nolde; ac ferde and wearp hyne on cweartern, oðþæt he hym eall agéfe. 31. Ða gesawon hys efen þeowas þæt, þa wurdon hig swyðe geûnrotsode, and comon and sædon heora hlaforde ealle þa dæde. 32. Ðâ clypode his hlaford hyne, and cwæð to him, Eala þu lyþra þeowa! ealne þinne gylt ic þe forgeaf, forþam þe ðu me bæde: 33. hu ne gebyrede þê gemiltsian þinum efen þeowan, swa swa ic þe gemiltsode? 34. Ða wæs se hlaford yrre, and sealde hyne þam wîtnerum, oðþæt he eall agulde. 35. Swa deð min se heofenlica Fæder, gyf gé of eowrum heortum eowrum broþrum ne forgyfað.

St. Matth. xx. 1–16.

Soðlice heofena rice ys gelic þam hyredes ealdre, þe on ærne mergen ût eode áhyrian wyrhtan on hys wín geard. 2. Gewordenre gecwydrædene þam wyrhtum, he sealde ælcon ænne penig wið hys dæges weorce: he asende hig on hys wîn geard. 3. And þa he ût eode ymbe undern tide, he geseah oþre on stræte idele standan: 4. þa cwæð he: Gâ gé on minne wîn geard, and ic sylle eow þæt riht byð: and hig þa ferdon. 5. Eft he ût eode ymbe þa sixtan and nigoþan tide, and dyde þam swâ gelîce. 6. Ða ymbe þa endlyftan tide he ût eode, and funde oþre standende, and þa sæde he: Hwi stande ge her ealne dæg idele? 7. Ða cwædon hig: Forþam þe ûs nan man ne hyrede. Ða cwæð he: And gâ gé on minne wîn geard. 8. Soðlice þa hyt wæs æfen geworden, þa sæde se wîn geardes hlaford his geréfan: Clypa þa wyrhtan, and agyf hym heora mede: agyn fram þam ytemestan oð ðone fyrmestan. 9. Eornestlice þa þa gecomon þe ymbe þa endlyftan tîde comon, þa onfengon hig ælc his

pening.   10. And þa þe þær ærest comon wendon þæt hig
sceoldon mare onfón ; þa onfengon hig syndrige penegas.
11. Ða ongunnon hig murcnian ongén þone hyredes
ealdor, and þus cwædon : 12. Ðas ytemestan worhton
âne tide, and þu dydest hig gelice us, þe bæron byrþena
on þyses dæges hætan.   13. Ða cwæð he andswariende
heora anum : Eala þu freond, ne dó ic þe nænne teonan :
hú ne come þu to me to wyrcanne wið anum peninge ?
14. nim þæt þín ys and ga : ic wylle þysum ytemestum
syllan eall swa mycel swa þe.   15. Oððe ne mot ic dón
þæt ic wylle ? hwæþer þe þin eage mánful ys, forþam þe
ic gód eom ?   16. Swa beoð þa fyrmestan ytemeste, and
þa ytemestan fyrmeste : soðlice manega synd geclypede,
and feawa gecorene.

St. Matth. xxii. 1–14.

Ða sæde he hym eft oðer bigspel, and þus cwæð :
2. Heofena rice ys gelic geworden þam cyninge þe
macode hys suna gifta : 3. and sende hys þeowas, and clypode þa gelaðodan to þam giftum : þa noldon hig cuman.
4. Ða sende he eft oðre þeowas, and sæde þam gelaðodon,
Nú ic gegearwode mine feorme : mine fearras and mine
fugelas synd ofslegene, and ealle mine þing synd gearwe :
cumað to þam giftum.   5. Ða forgymdon hig þæt, and
ferdon ; sum to hys tune, sum to hys mangunge.   6. And
ða oðre namon hys þeowas, and mid teonan geswencton,
and ofslogon.   7. Ða se cyning þæt gehyrde, þa wæs he
yrre, and sende hys here to, and fordyde þa man slagan,
and heora burh forbærnde.   8. Ða cwæð he to his þeowum,
Witodlice þas gyfta synd gearwe, ac ða þe gelaþode
wæron ne synd wyrþe.   9. Gað nú witodlice to wega

gelætum, and clypiað to þisum giftum swa hwylce swa ge gemeton. 10. Đa eodon ða þeowas út on þa wegas, and gegaderodon ealle þa þe hig gemetton, góde and yfele: þa wæron þa gyft hus mid sittendum mannum gefyllede. 11. Đa eode se cyning in, þæt he wolde geseon þa ðe þær sæton, þa geseah he þær ænne man þe næs mid gyftlicum reafe gescryd: 12. þa cwæð he, La freond, humeta eodest þu in, and næfdest gyftlic reaf? Đa gesuwode he. 13. And se cyning cwæð to hys þénum, Gebindað hys handa, and hys fet, and weorpað hyne on þa uttran þystro; þær byð wop and toþa gristbitung. 14. Witodlice manega synt gelaþode, and feawa gecorene.

St. Matth. xxv. 1–13.

Đys sceal to haligra fæmnena Mæsse-dæge.

Đonne byð heofena rice gelic þam tyn fæmnum, þe ða leoht fatu namon, and ferdon ongean þone brydguman and þa bryde. 2. Heora fif wæron dysege, and fif gleawe. 3. And þa fif dysegan namon leoht fatu, and ne namon nænne ele mid hym: 4. þa gleawan namon ele on heora fatum, mid þam leoht fatum: 5. Đa se bryd guma ylde, þa hnappedon hig ealle and slepon. 6. Witodlice to middere nihte man hrymde, and cwæð, Nu, se bryd guma cymð; farað him togeanes. 7. Đa aryson ealle þa fæmnan, and glengdon heora leoht fatu. 8. Đa cwædon þa dysegan to þam wisum, Syllað us of eowrum ele; forþam ure leoht fatu synd acwencte. 9. Đa andswaredon þa gleawan, and cwædon, Nese; þy læs þe we and ge nabbon genoh: gað to þam cypendum, and bycgað eow ele. 10. Witodlice þa hig ferdon, and woldon bycgan, þa com se bryd guma; and þa þe gearowe wæron, eodon in mid him to

þam giftum : and seo duru wæs belocen. 11. Ða æt
nehstan comon þa oðre fæmnan and cwædon, Dryhten,
Dryhten, læt ús in. 12. Ða andswarode he heom, and
cwæð, Soð ic eow secge, ne can ic eow. 13. Witodlice
waciað ; forþam ðe ge nyton ne þone dæg, ne þa tide.

St. Mark ii. 14-19.

And þa he forð eode, he geseah Leuin Alphei sittende
æt his cep setle, and he cwæð to hym : Folga mé. Ða
aras he and folgode hym. 15. And hit gewearð, þa he sæt
on his húse, þæt manega mánfulle sæton mid þam Hælende, and his leorning cnyhtum ; soðlice manega, þa ðe
hym fyligdon, wæron boceras and Pharisei, and cwædon :
16. Witodlice he ýtt mid mánfullum and synfullum, and hig
cwædon to hys leorning cnyhtum : Hwi ytt eower lareow
and drincð mid mánfullum and synfullum ? 17. Ða se
Hælend þys gehyrde, he sæde him : Ne beþurfon na
ða halan læces, ac ða þe untrume synd : ne com ic na
þæt ic clypode rihtwise, ac synfulle. 18. And þa wæron
Iohannes leorning cnyhtas and Pharisei fæstende : and
þa comon hig, and sædon hym : Hwi fæstað Iohannes
leorning cnyhtas and Phariseorum, and þine ne fæstað?
19. Ða cwæð se Hælend : Cweðe ge sculon þæs brydguman cnyhtas fæstan swa lange swa se bryd guma mid
him is ? ne magon hi fæstan swa lange tíde swa hig ðone
bryd guman mid hym habbað.

S. *Mark* iv. 1-20.

And eft he ongan hig æt ðære sǽ lǽran, and him
wæs mycel mænigeo to gegaderod, swa þæt he on scyp
eode, and on þære sǽ wæs ; and eall seo mænigeo ymbe

þa sǽ wæs, on lánde. 2. And he hig fela on bigspellum lærde, and him to cwæð on his lare : 3. Gehyrað ; Ut eode se sǽdere his sǽd to sawenne : 4. and þa he seow, sum feoll wið þone weg, and fugelas comon, and hit fræton. 5. Sum feoll ofer stan scylian, þar hit næfde mycele eorðan, and sona úp eode ; forþam hit næfde eorðan þiccnesse. 6. Ða hit úp eode, seo sunne hit forswælde, and hit forscranc ; forþam hyt wyrt ruman næfde. 7. And sum feoll on þornas ; þa stigon ða þornas, and forðrysmodon þæt, and hit wæstm ne bær. 8. And sum feoll on god land, and hit sealde, úp stigende and wexende, wæstm ; and án brohte þrytigfealdne, sum syxtigfealdne, sum hundfealdne. 9. And he cwæð ; Gehyre, se ðe earan hæbbe to gehyranne. 10. And þa he ana wæs, hine acsodon þæt bigspell þa twelfe þe mid him wæron. 11. And he sæde heom : Eow ys geseald to witanne Godes ríces gerýnu ; þam þe úte synd, ealle þing on bigspellum geweorþað : 12. þæt hig geseonde geseon, and na ne geseon ; and gehyrende gehyron, and ne ongiton ; þe læs hig hwænne syn gecyrrede, and heom syn hyra synna forgyfene. 13. Ða sæde he him : Ge nyton þis bigspell : and hu mage ge ealle bigspell witan ? 14. Se þe sæwð, word he sæwð. Soðlice þa synd wið þone weg, þar þæt word ys gesawen ; 15. and þonne hig hit gehyrað, sona cymð Satanas, and afyrð þæt word þe on heora heortan asawen ys. 16. And þa synd gelice þe synd ofer stan scylian gesawen : sona þonne hig þæt word gehyrað, and þæt mid blisse onfoð ; 17. and hig nabbað wyrt ruman on him, ac beoð unstaðolfæste ; and syððan up cymð deofles costnung, and his ehtnys for þam worde. 18. Hig synd on þornum gesawen ; þæt synd þa ðe þæt word gehyrað, 19. and of yrmðe, and swicdome worold welena, and oðra gewilnunga, þæt word

ofþrysmiað, and synd buton wæstme gewordene. 20. And
þa ðe gesawene synd ofer þæt gode land, þa synd þa þæt
word gehyrað, and onfoð, and wæstm bringað, sum þrytigfealdne, sum syxtigfealdne, and sum hundfealdne.

St. Mark vi. 1–11.

And þa he þanon eode, he ferde on his eþel, and him
folgedon hys leorning cnyhtas. 2. And gewordenum reste
dæge, he ongan on gesomnunge læran; and mænige
gehyrdon, and wundredon on his láre, and cwædon:
Hwanon synd þyssum ealle þas þing? and hwæt ys se
wisdom þe hym geseald ys, and swylce mihta þe þurh
his handa gewordene synd? 3. Hu nys þys se smið,
Marian sunu, Iacobes broðer, and Iosepes, and Iude,
and Simonis? hu ne synd hys swustra her mid ús?
And þa wurdon hig gedrefede. 4. Ða cwæð se Hælend:
Soðlice nys nán witega butan weorþscype, buton on his
eðele, and on his mægðe, and on his húse. 5. And he ne
mihte þar ænig mægen wyrcan, buton feawa untrume, on-
asettum his handum, he gehælde. 6. And he wundrode for
heora ungeleafan. He þa lærende, þa castel beferde.
7. And him twelfe to geclypode, and agan hig sendan,
twam and twam; and him anweald sealde unclænra
gasta; 8. and him bebead þæt hig naht on wege ne namon,
buton gyrde áne: ne codd, ne hlaf, ne feoh on heora
gyrdlum: 9. ac gesceode mid calcum; and þæt hig mid
twam tunecum gescrydde næron. 10. And he cwæð to
him: Swa hwylc hús swa ge in gað, wuniað þar, oð þæt ge
útgan, 11. And swa hwylce swa eow ne gehyrað, þonne
ge þanon út gað, ásceacað þæt dust of eowrum fotum,
him on gewitnesse.

St. Mark x. 17–31.

Ðys sceal on Wodnes dæg, on ðære seofeðan wucan
ofer Pentecosten.

And þa he on wege eode, sum him to arn, and
gebigedum cneowe to foran him, cwæð, and bæd hine:
La góda Lareow, hwæt do ic þæt ic éce lif age? 18. Ða
cwæð se Hælend: Hwi segst þu me godne? nys nan
mann gód, buton God ana. 19. Canst þu þa bebodu, Ne
unriht hæm þu, Ne slyh þu, Ne stel þu, Ne sege þu
lease gewitnesse, Facen ne do þu, Weorþa þinne fæder
and þine modor? 20. Ða answarede hé: Goda Lareow,
eall þis ic geheold of minre geoguþe. 21. Se Hælend
Hine þa behealdende, lufode, and sæde him: An þing þe
ys wana: gesyle eall þæt þu age, and syle hit þearfum;
þonne hæfst þu gold hord on heofenum; and cum, and
folga me. 22. And for þam worde he wæs geunret; and
ferde gnornigende; forþam he hæfde mycele æhta. 23. Ða
cwæð se Hælend to his leorning cnyhtum, hine beseonde:
Swyðe earfoðlice on Godes rice gað þa þe feoh habbað!
24. Ða forhtedon his leorning cnyhtas be his wordum.
Eft se Hælend him andswariende cwæð: Eala cild, swyðe
earfoðlice þa ðe on heora feo getruwiað gað on Godes
rice! 25. Eaþere ys olfende to farenne þurh nædle þyrel,
þonne se rica and se welega on Godes rice gá. 26. Hig
þæs þe ma betweox him wundredon, and cwædon: And
hwa mæg beon hal? 27. Ða beheold se Hælend hig, and
cwæð: Mid mannum hyt ys uneaþelic, ac na mid Gode:
Ealle þing mid Gode synt eaþelice. 28. Ða ongan Petrus
cweþan: Witodlice, we ealle þing forleton and folgodon
þe. 29. Ða andswarode him se Hælend: Nys nan þe hys
hus forlæt, oþþe gebroþru, oþþe geswustra, oþþe fæder,

oþþe moder, oþþe bearn, oþþe æceras, for me and for
þam godspelle, 30. þe hundfeald ne onfó nu on þysse tide,
hus, and broþru, and swustra, and fæder, and modor,
and bearn, and æceras, mid ehtnessum ; and on toweardre
worulde, éce lif. 31. Manega fyrmeste beoð ytemeste ;
and ytemeste, fyrmeste.

St. Mark xi. 1–10.

Ðys gebyrað feower wucon ær Myddan wyntran.

Ða he genealæhte Hierusalem, and Bethanía, to Oliuetes
dune, he sende hys twegen leorning cnyhtas, 2. and cwæð
to him : Farað to þam castelle, þe ongean ínc ys, and-
gyt þær sona gemetað assan folan getigedne, ofer þæne
nán man gyt ne sæt : ungetigeað hine, and to me ge-
lædað, 3. And gif hwa to ínc hwæt cwyð, secgað, Ðæt
Dryhten hæfð his neode ; and he hine sona hyder læt.
4. And þa hig út ferdon, hig gemetton þone folan úte on
twycinan beforan dura getigedne : þa untigdon hig hine.
5. And sume þe þar stodon, þus sædon him : Hwæt do
gyt, þone folan untigende ? 6. Ða cwædon hig : Swa se
Hælend unc bead : and hi leton hig þa. 7. Ða læddon
hig þone folan to þam Hælende, and hig heora. reaf
on áledon ; and he on sæt. 8. Manega heora reaf on
þone weg strehton : sume þa bogas of þam treowum
heowon, and streowedon on þone weg. 9. And þa ðe
beforan eodon, and þa ðe æfter folgodon, cwædon þus :
Osanná : Sy gebletsod se þe com on Dryhtnes naman :
10. Sy gebletsod þæt ríce þe com ures fæder Dauides :
Osanná on heahnessum.

St. Mark xii. 13–17.

Ðys sceal on ðære xxiiii wucan ofer Pentecosten.

Ða sendon hig to him sume of Phariseum and Herodianum, þæt hig befengon hine on his worde. 14. Ða comon hig, and þus mid facne cwædon: Láreow, we witon þæt þu eart soðfæst, and þu ne recst be ænegum men: ne besceawast þu manna ansyne; ac þu Godes weg lærst on soðfæstnysse: Alyfð gafol to syllanne þam Casere, hwæþer þe we ne syllað? 15. Ða cwæð he, and heora lotwrencas wiste: Hwi fandige ge mín, bringað mê þone pening, þæt ic hyne geseo. 16. Ða brohton hig hym. Ða sæde he hym: Hwæs ys þeos anlicnys, and þis gewrit? Hig cwædon: Þæs Caseres. 17. Ða cwæð se Hælend to hym. Agyfað þam Casere þa þing þe þæs Caseres synd, and Gode þa þe Godes synd. Ða wundredon hig be þam.

St. Mark xiii. 28–37.

Leorniað an bigspel be þam fic treowe: Þonne his twig bið mearu, and leaf beoð acennede, ge witon þæt sumor ys gehende: 29. and wite ge þonne ge þas þing geseoð, þæt he ys dura gehende. 30. Soðlice ic eow secge, þæt þeos cneores ne gewit, ærþam ealle þas þing geweorþon. 31. Heofen and eorðe gewitað; witodlice mine word ne gewitað. 32. Be þam dæge and þære tide nan man nat, ne englas on heofnum, ne mannes Sunu, buton Fæder ána. 33. Warniað, and waciað, and gebiddað eow; ge nyton hwænne seo tid ys. 34. Swa se man, þe ælþeodlice ferde, forlet his hus, and sealde his þeowum þone anweald gehwylces weorces, and beode þam dure wearde þæt he wacige. 35. Eornostlice waciað:

ge nyton hwænne þæs huses hlaford cymð, ðe on æfen, þe on midre nihte, þe on hancrede, þe on mergen: 36. þe læs he eow slæpende gemête, þonne he færinga cymð. 37. Soðlice ic eow secge, eallum ic hit secge, Waciað.

St. Luke i. 56–65.

Ðys gebyrað on Mid sumeres Mæsse dæg.

Soðlice María wunede mid hyre swylce þrý monðas, and gewende þa to· hyre huse. 57. Ða wæs gefylled Elizabethe cenning tíd, and heo sunu cende. 58. And hyre nehheburas and hyre cuðan þæt gehyrdon, þæt Dryhten hys mild heortnysse mid hyre mærsode, and hy mid hyre blissodon. 59. Ða on þam ehteoðan dæge hig comon þæt cild ymb sniðan; and nemdon hyne hys fæder naman Zachariam. 60. Ða andswarode hys moder: Nese soðes; ac he byð Iohannes genemned. 61. Ða cwædon hig to hyre: Nis nán on þínre mægðe þyson naman genemned. 62. Ða bycnodon hig to hys fæder, hwæt he wolde hyne genemnedne beón. 63. Ða wrát he, gebedenum wex brede, Iohannes ys hys nama. Ða wundredon hig ealle. 64. Ða wearð sona hys muð and his tunge geopenod, and he spræc, Drihten bletsiende. 65. Ða wearð ege geworden ofer eall hyra nehheburas; and ofer ealle Iudêa munt land wæron þas wórd gewidmærsode.

St. Luke ii. 36–50.

And Anna wæs witegestre, Fanueles dohtor, of Asséres mægðe: þeos wunede mænigne dæg, and heo lyfede mid hyre were seofen gear of hyre fæmnháde; 37. and heo wæs wuduwe oð feower and hund ehtatig geara, seo of þam temple ne gewat, dæges and nihtes þeowigende on fæstenum and on halsungum. 38. And þeos þǽre tíde becumende, Dryhtne andette, and be hym spræc eallum þam þe geanbidedon Hierusalem alysednysse. 39. And þa hig ealle þing gefyldon, æfter Dryhtnes ǽ, hig gehwurfon on Galileam, on heora ceastre Nazareth. 40. Soðlice þæt cild weox, and wæs gestrangod, wîsdomes full, and Godes gyfu wæs on hym. 41. And his magas férdon ælce gere to Hierusalem, on Easter dæges freols tîde. 42. And þa he wæs twelf wintre, hig fóron to Hierusalem, to þam Easterlican freolse, æfter heora gewunan. 43. And gefylledum dagum, þa hig ongean gehwurfon, belaf se Hælend on Hierusalem; and his magas þæt nyston : 44. wendon þæt he on heora gefére wǽre. Ða cómon hig ânes dæges fær, and hine sohton betweox his magas and his cuðan. 45. Ða hig hyne ne fundon, hig gewendon to Hierusalem, hine secende. 46. Ða æfter þrim dagum, hig fundon hine on þam temple, sittende on middan þam lareowum, hlystende and hig acsigende. 47. Ða wundredon hig ealle þe gehyrdon be his gleawscype and his andswarum.ᐧ 48. Ða cwæð his moder to hym : Sunu hwi dydest þu unc þus? þin fæder and ic sarigende þe sohton. 49. Ða cwæð he to hym : Hwæt ys þæt gyt me sohton? nyste gyt þæt me gebyrað to beonne on þam þingum þe mines Fæder synd? 50. Ða ne ongeaton hîg þæt wórd þe he to hym spræc.

St. Luke vi. 27–38.

Ac ic eow secge, forþam þe ge gehyrað, Lufiað eowre fynd, doð þam tala þe eow hatedon, 28. bletsiað þa ðe eow wirgeað, gebiddað for þa þe eow onhiscað. 29. And þam ðe þe slyhð on þîn gewenge wend oðer ongean ;

and þam ðe þín reaf nymð, ne forbeod hym na þíne tunecan. 30. Syle ælcum þe ðe bidde; and se ðe nimð þa þing þe þíne synd, ne mynga þu hyra. 31. And swa ge wyllað þæt eow men dón, doð hcom gelice. 32. And hwylc þanc ys eow, gif ge lufiað þa þe eow lufiað? soðlice synfulle lufiað þa ðe hig lufiað. 33. And gif ge wel doð þam ðe eow wel doð, hwylc þanc ys eow? witodlice·þæt doð synfulle. 34. And gif ge lænað þam þe ge eft æt onfoð, hwylc þanc ys eow? soðlice synfulle synfullum lænað, þæt hig gelíce onfón. 35. Ðeahhwæþre lufiað eowre fýnd, and hym wel doð, and læne syllað, nan þing þanun eft gehyhtende; and eower med byð mycel on heofone, and ge beoð þæs Hehstan bearn: forþam þe he ys gód ofer unþancfulle and ofer yfele. 36. Eornostlice beoð mild heorte, swa eower Fæder ys mild heort. 37. Nelle ge deman, and ge ne beoð demede: nelle ge genyðerian, and ge ne beoð genyðerode: forgyfað, and eow byð forgyfen: 38. sýllað, and eow byð geseald; gód gemét, and full, and geheapod, and oferflowende, hig syllað on eowerne bearm.

St. Luke xi. 1–13.

Soðlice wæs geworden, þa he wæs on sumere stowe hine gebiddende, þa ða he geswac, him to cwæð án his leorning cnyhta: Dryhten, lǽr ús ús gebiddan, swa Iohannes his leorning cnyhtas lærde. 2. Ða cwæð he to him: Cweðað þus, þonne ge eow gebiddað, Ure Fæder, þu þe on heofene eart, Sig þin nama gehalgod. Tó cume þin ríce. Geweorðe þin wylla on heofene, and on eorþan. 3. Syle us to dæg urne dæghwamlican hláf. 4. And forgyf us ure gyltas, swa we forgyfað ælcum þæra

þe wiðð us agylt. And ne læd þu us on costunge; ac
alýs ús fram yfele. 5. Ða cwæð he to him: Hwylc
eower hæfð sumne freond, and gæð to midre nihte to
him, and cwæð to him, La freond, læn me þry hlafas;
6. forþam mîn freond com of wêge to me, and ic næbbe
hwæt ic him to foran lecge; 7. and he þonne him þus
andswarige, Ne beo þu me gram: nu min duru ys
belocen, and mine cnyhtas synd on reste mid me; ne
mæg ic arîsan nú and syllan þe. 8. Gyf he þonne þurh-
wunað cnuciende, ic eow secge, gyf he [ne] aryst, and
him sylð þonne, forþam þe he his freond ys, þeah hwæðere
for his onhrope he aryst, and sylð him his neode. 9. And
ic eow secge: Biddað, and eow bið seald; secað, and ge
findað; cnuciað, and eow bið ontyned. 10. Ælc þæra
þe bitt onfehð; and se þe secð, he fint; and cnuciendum
byð ontyned. 11. Hwylc eower bitt his fæder hlafes,
segst þu sylð he him stán? oððe gif he bitt fîsces, sylð he
him næddran for fisce? 12. oððe gif he bitt æg, segst
þu ræcð he him scorpionem (þæt ys an wyrm cynn)?
13. Witodlice gyf ge þonne, þe synd yfele, cunnon
syllan góde sylene eowrum bearnum, swa mycele ma
cower Fæder on heofone sylð Godne Gast þam ðe hine
biddað.

S. Luke xv.

**Ðys Godspel sceal on ðone feorðan Sunnan dæg ofer
Pentecosten.**

Soðlice him genealæhton mánfulle and synfulle, þæt
hig his word gehyrdon. 2. Ða murcnedon þa Farisei and
þa boceras, and cwædon: Ðes onfehð synfulle, and mid
him ytt. 3. Ða cwæð he þis bigspel to þam: 4. Hwylc
man ys of eow þe hæfð hund sceapa, and gif he forlyst

H

ân of þam, hu ne forlæt he þonne nygon and hund nygon-
tig on þam westene, and gæð to þam ðe forwearð, oð he
hit fint? 5. And þonne he hit fint, he hit set on his exla
geblissiende. 6. And þonne he ham cymð, he to somne
clypað hys frynd and hys nehheburas, and cwyð, Blissiað
mid me; forþam ic funde min sceap þe for wearð. 7. ic
secge eow, þæt swa byð on heofone blis be anum synfullum þe dæd bote deð, ma þonne ofer nygon and
nygontigum.rihtwisra þe dæd bote ne beþurfon. 8. Oððe
hwylc wif hæfð tyn scyllingas, gif heo forlyst ænne
scylling, hu ne onælþ heo hyre leoht fæt, and awent hyre
hus, and secð geornliçe oð heo hine fint? 9. And þonne
heo hine fint, heo clypað hyre frynd and nehhebyryna,
and cwyð, Blissiað mid me; forþam ic funde minne
scylling þe ic forleas. 10. Ic secge eow, swa bið blis
beforan Godes englum be anum synfullum þe dæd bote
deð.

**Ðys Godspel gebyrað on Sæternes dæg, on ðære oðere
Lencten wucan.**

11. He cwæð: Soðlice sum man hæfde twegen suna.
12. Ða cwæð se yldra to his fæder, Fæder, syle me
minne dæl minre æhte þe me to gebyreð. Ða dælde he
hym hys æhte. 13. Ða, æfter feawa dagum, ealle his
þing gegaderode se gingra sunu, and ferde wræclice on
feorlen rîce, and forspilde þar his æhta, lybbende on his
gælsan. 14. Ða he hig hæfde ealle amyrrede, þa wearð
mycel hunger on þam rîce; and he wearð wædla. 15. Ða
ferde he and folgode ânum burh sittendum men þæs
rîces: þa sende he hine to his tune, þæt he heolde hys
swyn. 16. Ða gewilnode he his wambe gefyllan of þam
bean coddum þe ða swyn æton: and him man ne seaide.

St. John ix. 1-12.

Ðys Godspel gebyraÞ on Wodnes dæg, on Myd fæstenes wucan.

Ða se Hælend fór, þa geseah he ænne man þe wæs blind geboren. 2. And his leorning cnyhtas hyne acsedon, and cwædon: Láreow, hwæt syngode þes, oÞÞe his magas, þæt he wære blind geboren? 3. Se Hælend andswarode, and cwæÞ: Ne syngode he, ne his magas: ac þæt Godes weorc wære geswutelod on him. 4. Me gebyraÞ to wyrcanne þæs weorc þe me sende, þa hwyle þe hyt dæg ys: nyht cymÞ, þonne nan man wyrcan ne mæg. 5. Ic eom myddan eardes leoht, þa hwyle þe ic on myddan earde eom. 6. Ða he þas þing sæde, þa spætte he on þa eorþan, and worhte fenn of his spatle, and smyrede mid þam fenne ofer his eagan, 7. and cwæÞ to him: Gá, and þweh þe on Syloes mere. He fór, and þwoh hine, and com geseonde. 8. Witodlice hys neah geburas, and þa Þe hine gesawon, þa he wædla wæs, cwædon: Hu nis þis se þe sæt and wædlode? 9. Sume cwædon: He hyt is: sume cwædon: Nese, ac is him gelíc. He cwæÞ soÞlice: Ic hyt eom. 10. Ða cwædon hig to hym: Hu wæron þine eagan geopenede? 11. He andswarode, and cwæÞ: Se man þe is genemned Hælend worhte fenn, and smyrede mine eagan, and cwæÞ to me, Gá to Syloes mere, and þweh þe: and ic eode, and þwoh me, and geseah. 12. Ða cwædon hig to him: Hwar is he? Ða cwæÞ he: Ic nát.

St. John x. 1-21.

Ðys sceal on Tywes dæg, on Þære Pentecostenes wucan.

SoÞ ic secge eow, Se þe ne gæÞ æt þam geate in to sceapa falde, ac styhÞ elles ofer, he is þeof and sceaÞa.

2. Se þe in gæð æt þam geate, he is sceapა hyrde,
3. þæne se geat weard læt in, and þa sceap gehyrað his
stefne: and he nemð his agene sceap be naman, and
læt hig ût.   4. And þonne he his agene sceap læt ût, he
gæð beforan him, and þa sceap him fyliað; forþam þe
hig gecnawað his stefne.   5. Ne fyliað hig uncuþum, ac
fleoð fram him; forþam þe hig ne gecneowon úncuþra
stefne.   6. Ðis bigspel se Hælend him sæde: hig nyston
hwæt he spræc to him.   7. Eft se Hælend cwæð to him:
Soð ic eow secge: Ic eom sceapa geat.   8. Ealle þa ðe
comon wæron þeofas and sceaðan; ac þa sceap hig ne
gehyrdon.   9. Ic eom geat: swa hwylc swa þurh me
gæð, byð hal, and gæð in and ût, and fint læse.   10. Þeof
ne cymð, buton þæt he stele, and slea, and fordó: ic com
to þam þæt hig habbon lîf, and habbon genoh.

**Ðys sceal on Sunnan dæg, feowertyne nyht uppan
Eastron.**

11. Ic eom gód hýrde; gód hýrde sylð his lif for his
sceapum.   12. Se hýra, se ðe nis hýrde, and se þe nah
þa sceap, þonne he þone wulf gesyhð, þonne flyhð he,
and forlæt þa sceap: and se wulf nimð, and todrifð þa
sceap.   13. Se hýra flyhð, forþam þe he bið ahýrod,
and hym ne gebyrað to þam sceapum.   14. Ic eom gód
hýrde, and ic gecnawe mine sceap, and hig gecnawað me.
15. Swa min Fæder can me, ic can minne Fæder; and
ic sylle min agen lif for minum sceapum.   16. And ic
hæbbe oðre sceap, þa ne synt of þisse heorde; and hyt
gebyrað þæt ic ' læde þa, and hig gehyrað mine stefne;
and hyt byð an heord, and an hyrde.   17. Forþam
Fæder me lufað, forþam þe ic sylle mîne sawle, and hig
eft nime.   18. Ne nimð hig nan man æt me, ac læte hig

fram me sylfum. Ic hæbbe anweald míne sawle to alætanne, and ic hæbbe anweald hig eft to nimanne. Þis bebod ic nam æt minum Fæder. 19. Eft wæs ungeþwærnes geworden betweox þam Iudeum, for þysum spræcum. 20. Manega heora cwædon, Deofol ys on hym, and he wêt; hwi hlyste ge hym? 21. Sume cwædon, Ne synd na þys wodes mannes word. Cwyst þu mæg wód man blindra manna eagan ontynan?

St. John xi. 1–16.

Ðys sceal on Fryge dæg, on Myd fæstenes wucan.

Witodlice sum seoc man wæs genemned Lazarus, of Bethanía, of Marian ceastre and of Marthan, hys swustra. 2. Hyt wæs seó María þe smyrede Dryhten mid þære sealfe, and drigde his fet mid hyre loccum. Lazarus hyre broðer was geyflod. 3. Hys swustra sendon to hym, and cwædon : Dryhten, nu ys seoc se þe þu·lufast. 4. Ða se Hælend þæt gehyrde, þa cwæð he to him : Nys þeos untrumnys na for deaðe, ac for Godes wuldre; þæt Godes Sunu sig gewuldrod þurh hyne. 5. Soðlice se Hælend lufode Marthan and hyre swustor Marían, and Lazarum heora broðer. 6. Witodlice he wæs twegen dagas on þære sylfan stowe, þa he gehyrde þæt he seoc wæs. 7. Æfter þyssum he cwæð to hys leorning cnyhtum : Uton faran eft to Iudea lande. 8. Hys leorning cnyhtas cwædon to hym : Láreow, nu þa Iudeas sohton þe, þæt hig woldon þe hænan; and wylt þu eft faran þyder? 9. Se Hælend hym andswarode, and cwæð : Hu ne synd twelf tida þæs dæges? Gif hwa gæð on dæg, ne ætspyrnð he, forþam he gesyhð þyses middan eardes leoht. 10. Gif he gæð on niht, he ætspyrnð, forþam þe þæt leoht nys

on hyre.　11. Þas þing he cwæð : and syððan he cwæð
to him : Lazarus ure freond slæpð ; ac ic wylle gán,
and awreccan hyne of slæpe.　12. His leorning cnyhtas
cwædon: Dryhten, gif he slæpð, he byð hal.　13. Se
Hælend hit cwæð be his deaðe : hig wendon soðlice þæt
he hyt sæde be swefnes slæpe.　14. Ða cwæð se Hælend
openlice to him : Lazarus ys dead ; 15. and ic eom bliðe
for eowrum þingum, þæt ge gelýfon, forþam ic næs þara :
ac uton gán to him.　16. Ða cwæð Thomas to hys ge-
ferum : Uton gan, and sweltan mid him.

St. John xxi. 19–25.

**Ðys Godspel gebyrað on Sce Johannis Euangelista
mæsse dæg.**

And þa he þæt sæde, þa cwæð he to him : Fylig me.
20. ða Petrus hine bewende, þa geseah he þæt se leorning
cnyht him fyligde, þe se Hælend lufode ; se þe hlinode on
gebeorscipe ofer his breost, and cwæð, Dryhten, hwæt
ys se þe ðé belæwð ?　21. Witodlice þa Petrus þysne geseah,
þa cwæð he to þam Hælende : Dryhten, hwæt sceal þes ?
22. ða cwæð se Hælend to hym : Ic wylle þæt he wunige
þus oð ic cume : hwæt to þe ? fylig þu me.　23. Witodlice
þeos spræc cóm út gemang broðrum, þæt se leorning
cnyht ne swylt : and ne cwæð se Hælend to him, Ne
swylt he ; ac, Ðus ic wylle, þæt he wunige oð ic cume :
hwæt to þe ?　24. Ðys ys se leorning cnyht þe cyð gewitnesse be þyson, and wrat þas þing : and we witon þæt
hys gewitnes ys soð.　25. Witodlice oðre manega þing
synd þe se Hælend worhte : gif þa ealle awritene wæron, ic
wene ne mihte þes middan eard ealle þa bec befon.

A PARSING GLOSSARY.

Of the first two pieces every word is parsed in this Glossary; and where a single Numeral follows the Head-word, it refers to a line in them. After the Parsing comes a reference to the divisions of this Grammar; then the modern English equivalent; and lastly the numbers of other lines in which the same word recurs.—Additional references are made by chapter and verse.

ac 15. Conjunction ix. 2 :—*but*.

acsiað 25. Weak verb acsian, Imperative 2 pl. vi. 2 c:—*ask ye*.

acwencte Mt. xxv. 8. Weak vb. cwencan = *quench*. Past. Part. pl. :—*extinguished*.

ǽlcon Mt. xx. 2. = Dat. sing. masc. ǽlcum; of ǽlc; Indef. Pron. viii. 6 :—*to each*.

ǽnne Mt. xx. 2. Acc. sg. masc. of the Numeral án—p. 45 :—*one*.

ǽrne Mt. xx. 1. Acc. sg. masc. str. decl. of Adj. ǽr *early*; governed by on.

æt 11. Prep. with dat. On the use of this preposition with person-words, see x. 11 § 2 :—*at*.

águlde Mt. xviii. 34. Subj. Pret. 3 Pers. sg. á-geldan str. vb. p. 18 :—*should pay*.

áhte Mt. xviii. 25. See Præt.-Present verbs vi. 2 :—*owned*.

Alphei Mk. ii. 14. Genitive of *Alpheus* in its Latin form.

and 4. Conjunction ix. 2 ; *and*.

ánum Mt. xx. 13. Dat. sg. masc. án :—*to one*.

astrehte Mt. xviii. 26. Weak vb. streccan, 3 sing. pret. :— *he prostrated* (*himself*).

áwecceað 19. Weak vb. Im-

perative 2 pl. compound, á-weccean, xi. 2—*awake ye*.

bebeódende 13. Pres. part. of bebeódan compound of beó-dan, strong vb. vi. 1 :—*commanding*.

be-ferde Mk. vi. 6: *fared, travelled, round*.

beseónde (hine) Mk. x. 23. Pres. Part. of be-seón—with reflexive pronoun :— *looking around him*(*self*).

bidde, 11. Of biddan, vi. 1. subj. pres. 3rd sing. :—*ask*.

bigspell Mk. iv. 13. For bispell *parable*. In this verse the word occurs both in the singular and in the plural; and the form is the same in both instances, because it is a neuter strong substantive : vii. 1 γ.

bigyrdlum 22. Dat. pl. bigyrdel, *what hangs at the girdle, a purse*.

bodiað 18. Weak verb bodian, Imperative pl. vi. 2 c :—*preach ye*.

borgian 11. Weak verb vi. 2 c, infinitive :—*borrow*.

burh 24. Strong subst. fem. Acc. sing. vii. 1 β :—*fort, borough, city*.

byrþena Mt. xx. 12. Acc. pl.

str. sb. fem. byrþen, vii. 1 β:
—*burthens*.

byð 2 twice. Symbol-verb vi. 1 ;
3 sing. indic. pres. or future,
x. 2 a :—*is, shall be*, 29. 30
twice.

castel Mk. vi. 6. The Latin
castellum village. Acc. pl. nt.

ceastre 15. Strong subst. fem.
Dat. sing. vii. 1 β:—*city*.

ceastre 25. Acc. sing. *id*.

cíld Mt. xviii. 25. Plural neut.
vii. 1 γ:—*children*.

clænsiað 19. Weak vb. clæn-
sian, Imperative 2 pl. vi. 2 c :
—*cleanse ye*.

cneowe Mk. x. 17. Instr. case
of cneow, strong sb. neut. :—
knee.

codd 22. *bag, wallet*. Lk. xv. 16.

cwæþ 17. Pret. 3 sing. of cweðan, vi. 1 :—*said*.

cweðe ge Mk. ii. 19. This
phrase *Say ye* is used as a
formula of Interrogation.

cweþende 14. Part. pres. sing.
of cweðan, vi. 1 :—*saying*.

cweþende 18. Plural nom. of
the same, vii. 2 :—*saying*. 27.

cymþ 29. Strong vb. cuman vi.
1 : Indic. 3 Pres. used as Future x. 2 :—*cometh, shall come*.

dæd-bote Lk. xv. 7. Deed-
bettering, amends, repentance.
Genitive case governed by beþurfon.

deade 19. Strong adj. Acc. pl.
vii. 2 :—*dead*.

deoflu 20. Strong subst. neut.
Acc. pl. vii. 1 γ:—*devils*.

déð Mt. xviii. 35. Indic. Pres.
3 sg. of vb. dón vi. 1 fin. in
Future sense :—*he will do*.

dome 7. Subst. strong masc.
dat. sing. vii. 1 a :—*law*.

dóð 5. Verb don vi. 1 fin. Indic. pres. 3 pl. :—*they do*.

drífað 20. Strong verb drífan
vi. 1. Imperat. 2 pl. :—*drive*
(*ye*).

eáge 3. Weak subst. neut. nom.
vii. 1 א:—*eye*.

eáge 4. Accusative of same.

ealdre Mt. xx. 1. Dat. sg. str.
sb. masc. ealdor *master, chief*.

earfoð-líc-e Mk. x. 23; *hardly*.

eóde Mt. xx. 1. Weak Preterite
of str. vb. gán or gangan, p.
18:—*he went*.

eornost-líc-e Mk. xiii. 35.
Earnestly, verily, therefore.

eów 4. Pron. 2 Pers. Dat. pl.
viii. 1 :—*you*. 5. 30.

eówer 1. Gen. pl. of 2nd Pers.
pron. used as Possessive pronoun. viii. 1 and 2 :—*your*, 29.
30.

eówrum 22. Dat. pl. of eówer,
viii. 2 :—*your*.

éþel Mk. vi. 1 :—*native country*.

éþele Mk. vi. 4. Dative of same.

fare 14. Imperative pl. of faran
to go : a form used when ge
follows it. vi. 1 :—*go ye*.

fearras Mt. xxii. 4. Nom. pl.
str. masc. fear *ox*.

feóh 21. Strong subst. neut. Acc.
sing. vii. 1 γ § 1 :—*money*,
" fee."

feorme Mt. xxii. 4. Acc. sg.
fem. :—*dinner, banquet*.

flítan 8. Strong verb infin. vi.
1 :—*contend*.

folga Mk. ii. 14. Weak vb.
Imperative sing. :—*follow*.

for 4. Prep. with Acc. case ix.
1 :—*for*.

forscranc Mk. iv. 6. Strong
vb. for-scrincan, 3 pret. vi.
1 :—*it shrank, shrivelled up*.

forswélde Mk. iv. 6. Weak

vb. 3 pret. of for-swǽlan, vi.
2 a :—*burnt up, scorched.*
forwurdon 16. Pret. 3 pl. of
for-weorðan to perish, a compound of weorðan vi. 1.:—
have gone to ruin.
frǽton Mk. iv. 4. Strong vb.
3 pl. Pret. of frete, vi. 1 :—
they devoured.
fugelas Mt. xxii. 4. This rendering *fowls* must be due to a
confusion of the Latin *altilia*
fatlings, with *alites* birds.
funde Mt. xx. 6. See vi. 1, p.
25 :—*he found.*

gá 10. Imperative 2 sing. of
gan :—*go* (thou).
gá 14. Imperative 2 pl. of gan,
of a form used when ge follows :—*go* (*ye*). Mt. xx. 4.
gáð 15. Imperative 2 pl. of
gangan vi. 1 .—*go ye.* 17.
ge 3. Pron. 2nd pers. pl. nom. ;
viii. 1 :—*ye.* 14 twice. 20. 25.
26.
gearwe Mt. xxii. 8. Strong
adj. pl. nom. of gearo, *ready.*
vii. 2.
gebiddan (us, hine) Lk. xi. 1.
This vb. which signifies *to
pray,* mostly takes a reflexive
pronoun with it, as twice in
this verse.
gebigedum Mk. x. 17 (*i* for *y*).
Dat. sing. Past Part. of weak
vb. gebýgan, to bow, derived
from strong vb. búgan :—
with bended (*knee*).
gecweden 3. Participle past
of strong verb cweðan ; vi.
1 :—*said.*
gecyrred 31. Weak vb. ge-
cyrran, Participle past :—*returned.*
gedréfede Mk. vi. 3. Past
Participle plural of gedréfan.
Weak vb. vi. 2 a :—*troubled.*

gegearwa 6. Weak vb. gegear-
wian ; imperative 2nd pers.
sing. vi. 2 c :—*prepare, offer.*
gehýrdon 3. Weak vb. hýran ;
pl. pret. with Perfect sense, x.
2 a :—*heard, have heard.*
gelǽtum Mt. xxii. 9. Dat. pl. in
the phrase to wega gelǽtum
*to the outlets, openings, meet-
ings, of the roads.*
gelaðodan Mt. xxii. 3. Acc. pl.
wk. decl. of participle gelaðod
with Art. Def.:—*the* (*persons*)
invited.
gelaðodon Mt. xxii. 4. Dat. pl.
of participle gelaðod, for ge-
laðodum:—*to the invited ones.*
ge-líc Mt. xx. 1. Adj. str. neut.
nom. agreeing with ríce :—
like, ᵹleich.
genealǽcþ 18. Weak verb. ge-
nealǽcan, 3 sing. pres. indic. :
Compound xi. 2 :—*approaches.*
genýt 9. Weak verb genýdan,
3 sing. pres. ind. :—*compelleth.*
gerad Mt. xviii. 24. Strong
subst. neut. :—*reckoning.*
geradegode Mt. xviii. 23. Weak
vb. gerad(eg)ian, where -eg
is excrescent and to be pron.
as y ; 3 sing. pret. ind. :—
called to account.
gescý 23. Collective of sceó
shoe, xi. 1 :—*shoes, a pair of
shoes.*
ge-wíd-mǽrsod-e Lk. i. 65.
Pl. participle agreeing with
pl. word. The verb mǽrsian
= *make* mǽre *famous* ; and
-wíd- is *widely* :—*celebrated,
noised abroad.*
gewordenre Mt. xx. 2. Dat.
fem. str. adjectival decl. of
participle geworden (p. 23)
in concord with the subst.
gecwyd-rǽdene ; the whole
forming a pendent structure,
like the Latin Ablative Abso-

lute, of which indeed it is an imitation (conventione facta): —*a bargain having been made.* Examples of the same structure with other Gender or Number:—Mk. vi. 2, 5. Lk. i. 63.

gifta Mt. xxii. 2. Pl. acc. fem.: —*marriage.*

gife 20. See to gife.

gold 21. Strong subst. neut. Acc. sing. vii. 1 γ § 1:—*gold.*

grétaꝥ 27. Weak vb. Imperative 2 pl.:—*greet, salute ye.*

gyf (= gif) 2. Conjunction ix. 2:—*if.* 5. 28. 29.

gyft-hus Mt. xxii. 10. Compound Pl. nom. neut. vii. 1 γ:—*the nuptial houses or chambers.*

gyrde 23. Strong subst. fem. **gyrd,** Acc. sing. vii. 1 β:— *staff,* yard.

hǽlaꝥ 19. Weak vb. hǽlan, Imperative 2 pl. :—*heal ye.*

Hǽlend 13. Participial subst. of hǽlan to heal vi. 2 a:— *Healer,* Jesus. Jn. ix. 11.

hǽtan Mt. xx. 12. Dat. sg. of hǽte, wk. sb. vii. 1 א:—*heat.*

heofena 18. Strong subst. masc. Gen. pl. vii 1 a:—*of heavens.*

Herodianum Mk. xii. 13. Dat. pl. in Saxon form.

him 8. \Pron. 3ʳᵈ pers. masc. dat. sing. viii. 1 :—*to him.* Again 10.

him Mk. vi. 7. Pronoun Reflexive, x. 7:—*to himself.*

him (hym) Mk. ii. 17, 19. Dat. pl. :—*to them.*

hit 27. Pron. 3 Pers. neut. Acc.; viii. 1 :—*it.*

hiwrǽdene 16. Strong subst. fem. Gen. sing. vii. 1 β ; a Compound, xi. 2:—*of the family.*

hreofle 19. Strong adj. hreofl Acc. pl. vii. 2:—*leprous.*

hú Mk. vi. 3. Pron. Adv. Interrog. p. 50:—*how?* The phrase Hú nis is used to express *Is not?*

hús 27. Strong subst. neut. Acc. sing. vii. 1 γ:—*house.*

—— Nom. singular, 28.

húse 28. Dat. sing.

hwá 6. Pron. Indef. viii. 6 :— *any one.*

hwá 25. Pronoun Interrogative, viii. 5:—*who?*

hwanon Mk. vi. 2. Pron. Adv. Interrog. p. 53:—*whence.*

hwylce 24. Pron. Indef. Strong acc. fem. See swa hwylce.

hym (= him) 6. Pron. 3 Pers. dat. sing. masc. viii. 1 :—*to him.* 12.

hym (= heom) 13. Dat. pl. 3. Pron. Pers. viii. 1 :—*to them.*

hys (= his) 17. Gen. sing. viii. 1 :—*his.* 24.

hyt 1. = hit. Pron. 3ʳᵈ pers. Neut. nom. viii. 1 :—*it.* 29.

—— the same, accusative, 29.

ic 4. Pron. 1ˢᵗ Pers. sing. viii. 1 :—*I.*

ídele Mt. xx. 3. Str. pl. aj. **ídel** :—*idle.*

in-gán 27. Subj. Pres. pl. governed by þonne :—*ye go in.*

in-gáꝥ 25. Compound of gán or gangan, vi. 1. Indic. pres. 2 pl. :—*ye go in.*

innan 15. Prep. gov. dative ; ix. 1 :—*within.*

Israhela 16. A gen. pl. like Samaritana :—*of Israel.*

Lá Mk. x. 17. Interj. :—*Oh!*

lǽces Mk. ii. 17. Genitive of lǽce *physician* after beþurfon.

lǽt 8. Strong verb imperative ; vi. 1 :—*let, leave.*

leoht-fatu Mt. xxv. 3. Compound of leoht *light*, and fatu pl. of fæt *vessel*, vii. 1 γ:—*lamps*.

leorning-cnyhtum 17. Compound subst. xi. 2 ; strong Decl. masc. Dat. pl. vii. 1 *a* :—*disciples*.

Leuin Mk. ii. 14. Acc. of *Levi* in its Greek form.

má 15. Adverbial comparative of micel, vii. 2 :—*more, rather*.

mægen Mk. vi. 5. Strong sb. neut. :—*power, mighty work*.

mægðe Mk. vi. 4. Dat. sing. of mægð, strong sb. fem. :—*family*.

manega Mt. xx. 16. Indef. Pron. viii. 6 :—*many*. Mt. xxii. 14 ; Mk. ii. 15.

mánful Mt. xx. 15. Aj. neut. nom. in concord with eáge vii. 1 𐍃 :—*wicked, evil* (*eye*). The st. pl. in Mk. ii. 15, 16, where it means the Publicans.

mangunge Mt. xxii. 5. Dat. sg. of str. fem. mangung *commerce*.

mare 2. Adj. Comparative neut. of micel, vii. 2 :—*more*.

metes 24. Strong subst. masc. mete, Gen. sing. vii. 1 *a* :—*meat*.

mid 10. Prep. with dat. ix. 1 :—*with*.

mín Mk. xii. 15. Gen. sg. of ic after vb. fandian *try, tempt, prove* : p. 59.

minne Mt. xx. 4. Acc. masc. of Pron. Pos. mín, viii. 2 :—*my*.

næbbe ge 21. Negative of habban vi. 2 d and x. 12 ; Imperative pl. :—*do ye not have*.

næfde Mt. xviii. 25 : = ne hæfde, vi. 2 (d) :—*had not*.

ne 5. Verbal negative, x. 10 :—*not*. 11. 14 twice. 30.

né 21 twice. Conjunctional negative, x. 12 :—*nor*. 22 twice. 23 twice.

nese Mt. xxv. 9. The opposite of gese *yes* :—*not so, nay*.

niman 8. Strong verb infinitive ; vi. 1 :—*take*.

nys (= nis) 2. Coalition of ne and is ; x. 12 :—*is not*.

nyton (= ne witon) Mt. xxv. 13 :—*ye know not*.

óð 26. Conjunction, ix. 2 :—*until*.

of 3. Preposition gov. Dative, ix. 1 :—*from, out of*.

ofer 29. Preposition gov. Acc. ix. 1 :—*over, upon*.

on 14. Prep. with Acc. x. 11 § 2 :—*into*. 24. 27.

on 6. Prep. with acc. ix. 1 :—*on*.

on 7. With dat. :—*in*. 22 tw. 25.

onfengon 20. Compound of strong vb. fangan vi. 1 : Pret. 2 pl. :—*ye have received*.

ongén (= ongeán) 5. Prep. governing acc. ix. 1 :—*against*.

óðer 7. Pron. Indef. viii. 6 :—*other*.

óðre 10. Plural of óðer.

óððe 24. Conjunction ix. 2 :—*or*.

peninge Mt. xx. 13. Dat. of pening after prep. wið, x. 11 § 1 :—*for a penny*.

Phariseum Mk. xii. 13. Dat. pl. in Saxon form.

ríce 18. Strong subst. neut. Nom. sing. vii. 1 γ § 2 :—*kingdom*.

Samaritana 15. Gen. pl. formed from the Latin *Samaritan-orum* by changing the Latin genitival inflection *-orum* for the Saxon equivalent *-a*, according to the Declensions of Strong Substantives: vii. 1 : —*of Samaritans.*

sceal. In the Rubrical headings **Dis sceal to** *This belongs to,* This is the proper lesson for such a Tide. See p. 10.

sceapum 16. Strong subst. neut. dat. pl. vii. 1 γ :—(*to the*) *sheep.*

sceolde Mt. xviii. 24. One of the Præt. Præs. vbs. vi. 2 :—*owed.*

se 13. Pronoun Demonstrative as Def. Article, masc. sing. nom. viii. 3 :—*the.* 16. 23.

sealde Mt. xx. 2. Weak vb. vi. 2 (a), p. 28 :—*he gave.*

secge 4. Wk. vb. 1 Pres. Indic. vi. 2 d :—*I say.*

sende 13. Preterite of **sendan** : —*he sent.*

sleá 6. Strong verb **sleán** vi. 1 ; Subj. pres. 3 sing. :—*smite.*

slépon, Mt. xxv. 5. Strong vb. **slápan,** Indic. Pret. 3 pl. :— *they slept.*

sóðes Lk. i. 60. Str. Gen. aj. **sóð** *true,* used adverbially :— *of a truth, verily.*

sóðlice 1. Adverb used conjunctionally : — *verily, truly, however, but.* 2. 4. 23. 27. 30.

spréc 1. Strong subst. fem. Nom. sing. :—*speech.*

standan Mt. xx. 3. Strong vb. (vi. 1) Infin. Mood after **ge-seah** :—*he saw standing.*

stan-scylian Mk. iv. 5. Weak sb. fem. Dat. of **scylie,** vii. 1 א :—*stone-crag.*

stapa 9. Strong subst. masc. gen. pl. :—*of steps.*

swá 25. Relative to Antecedent **swá hwylce,** which see.

swá hwá swá 9. Pron. Indef. viii. 6 :—*whosoever.*

swá hwylce 24. A phrasal Indefinite Pronoun ; viii. 6 :— *whichsoever, whatsoever.*

swustra Mk. vi. 3 pl. nom. ; vii. 1 § :—*sisters.*

swiðre 6. Adj. Comparative neut. acc. sing. weak Declension vii. 2 :—*stronger, right.*

sý 1. 3 pers. sing. pres. subj. of verb *to be,* used as a gentle imperative : *be it, let it be,* 28.

sý 25. Same word used subjunctively ; vi. 1 :—*may be.*

syb 28 = **sib.** Strong subst. fem. nom. sing. ; vii. 1 β :—*peace, friendship,* 29. 30.

syle 10. Verb weak **syllan** vi. 2 a, imperative 2 pers. :— *give.*

sylle Mt. xx. 4. First Pers. Indic. Pres. with Future sense, x. 2 a :—*I will give.*

syndrige Mt. xx. 10. Pl. acc. of **syndrig,** viii. 6, p. 52 :— *separate, several.* The expression **syndrige penegas** is imitative of the Latin *singulos denarios* = a penny severally, a penny each.

synna Mk. iv. 12. Pl. of **synn** *sin,* str. fem.

ticcen Lk. xv. 29 : *a kid of the goats.* Ziegchen.

tide Mt. xx. 5. Acc. str. fem. sb. **tíd,** vii. 1 β :—*time, hour.* Mt. xxv. 13.

tó 15. Prep. governing Dative ix. 1 :—*to.* 17. 30.

tó 8. Adverb :—*too, also, likewise.*

tó gife 20. Phrasal Adverb :— *as a gift, freely,* 21.

tóð 4 twice. Strong subst. masc. nom. and acc. vii. 1 § :—*tooth.*

túne Mt. xxii. 5. Dat. sg. of str. masc. tún *farm.*

tunecan 8. Subst. weak fem. sing. acc. ; vii. 1 א:—*coat.*

tunecan 23. Pl. same :—*coats.*

twá 10. Numeral cardinal ; vii. § :—*two.* 22.

twelf 13. Numeral Card. vii. § : —*twelve.*

twycinan Mk. xi. 4. Sb. weak fem. Dat. case ; from twi-cine = "two-chine," a place where roads split.

undern-tíde Mt. xx. 3. Undern = un-dark, i.e. full daylight, stood for the 3rd hour or 9 a.m. : tíde, str. sb. fem. acc. vii. 1 β :—*early fore-noon.*

unstaðolfæste Mk. iv. 17. Pl. str. of aj. un-staðol-fæst *not fast or firm in their foundation.*

untrume 19. Strong Adj. acc. pl. vii. 2 :—*un-strong, sick.*

út 20. Adverb vii. 2 :—*out.*

út-gán 26. Compound of gán or gangan : xi. 2 : Subj. pres. 2 pl. :—*ye go out.*

wæfels 9. Subst. strong masc. acc. :—*cloak.*

weg 14. Strong subst. masc. acc. sing. vii. 1 a :—*way.*

wege 22. Dat. sing. of weg.

weorce Mt. xx. 2. Dat. of str. subst. weorc, gov. by prep. wið—x. 11 § 1 :—*against* or *for his day's work.*

wenge 6. Strong subst. neut. acc. sing. vii. 1 γ § 2 :—*cheek.*

wét Jn. x. 20. Syncopate 3 sing. pres. Ind. of wédan (to be wód *mad*), wk. vb. vi. 2 a :— *he is mad.*

wæs 3. Symbol-verb; Indic. Pret. third pers. sing. vi. 1 :— *was, has been.*

winne 5. Strong verb winnan vi. 1, Imperative pl. 2nd person :—*strive ye.*

wítnerum Mt. xviii. 34. Dat. pl. of wítnere *tormentor, executioner,* str. subst. masc. vii. 1 a.

wið 7. Prep. with acc.; x. 11 § 1 :—*against.*

witodlice 28. Adverb vii. 3. used as a conjunction :—*verily, indeed, however.*

wucan Mk. x. 17 Rubric. Dat. sg. of wuce, sb. weak fem. :— *week.*

wuniað 26. Weak verb wunian, Imperative 2 pl. vi. 2 c :— *dwell ye.*

wyle 7. Verb willan, 3 pers. sing. pres. vi. 2 :—*will.*

wylle (= wille) 11. Of willan vi. 2. subj. pres. 3 sing. :— *will.*

wyrhta 23. Weak subst. masc. Nom. sing. vii. 1 א :—*wright, workman.*

wyrhtum Mt. xx. 2. Dat. pl. wyrhta.

wyrn 11. Of wyrnan weak verb, imperative 2nd pers. sing.: —*refuse.*

wyrðe 24. Adj. strong Nom. sing. masc. vii. 2 :—*worthy.* 25.

—— neuter nom. sing. 29. 30.

yfel 5. Either Strong adj. neut. acc. vii. 2 or Strong subst. neut. vii. 1 γ :—*evil.*

yfele 3. Dative of same.

ys (= is) 1 twice. Third sing. Pres. Ind. of verb *to be* : vi. 1 :—*is.* 23.

ytt Mk. ii. 16. Syncopate 3 sing. Pres. Indic. of etan vi. 1 : —*he eateth.*

þá 5. Pron. Demonstrative acc. pl. viii. 3 :—*those.*

ðá Mt. xx. 12. Conjunction :— *Then.*

þǽr 26. Adverb of place viii. 3. § :—*there.*

þǽre 26. Pron. Dem. Dat. fem. viii. 3. referring to the subst. fem. burh or ceastre, and governed by the prep. on : on þǽre = *in that (city).*

þæt 2. Pron. Demonstrative neut. nom. sing. viii. 3 :—*that.*

þæt 7. Def. Art. neut. viii. 3 :— *the.* 27. 28.

—— 3. Conjunction ix. 2 :— *that.* 18.

þam 7. Pron. Dem. masc. dat. sing. viii. 3 ; antecedent to ðe viii. 4 :—*to that* (person). 10. 11.

þam 15. Pron. Dem. dat. pl.; Antecedent to þe ; viii. 3:— *to those.*

þár 2. Adv. of place, same as þǽr viii. § :—*there.*

þás 13. Pron. Dem. þes, acc. pl. viii. 3 :—*these.*

ðe 5. Pron. Rel. Indecl. viii. 4 : —*who, which, that.* 11. 16.

þe 6. Pron. 2 Pers. Sing. acc. ; viii. 1 :—*thee.* 7. 9. 10.

þe 11. Dative of same.

þénum Mt. xxii. 13. Dat. pl. for þegenum or þegnum *thanes, servants.*

þeóda 14. Strong subst. fem. gen. pl. vii. 1 β :—*of nations,* i.e. of the Gentiles.

þín 6. Pron. Poss. 2nd pers. Sing. acc. neut. of strong adj. declension, viii. 2 : — *thine, thy.*

þíne 8. Of þín, acc. fem. sing.; vii. 2 :—*thy.*

þíne Mk. ii. 18. Nom. pl. of Poss. Pron. þín, viii. 2 :— *thine.*

þínne 8. Of þín, acc. masc. sing. viii. 2 :—*thy.*

þonne 26. Conjunction, ix. 2 :— *when.*

þing, things. It is a plural neuter, vii. 1 γ. Mt. xxii. 4.

þu 12. Pron. Pers. 2 sing. nom. viii. 1 :—*thou.*

þusend 9. Numeral cardinal with Genitive :—*a thousand.* 10.

þysum 28 = þisum. Pron. Demonst. Dat. sing. neut. viii. 3 :—*this.*

THE END.